THE OXFORD ANTHOLOGY OF

MODERN INDIAN POETRY

DATE DUE

GAYLORD · PRINTED IN U.S.A.

THE OXFORD ANTHOLOGY OF
MODERN INDIAN POETRY

edited by
VINAY DHARWADKER
and
A.K. RAMANUJAN

DELHI
OXFORD UNIVERSITY PRESS
CALCUTTA   CHENNAI   MUMBAI

Oxford University Press, Walton Street, Oxford OX2 6DP

Oxford   New York
Athens   Auckland   Bangkok   Calcutta
Cape Town   Chennai   Dar es Salaam   Delhi
Florence   Hong Kong   Istanbul   Karachi
Kuala Lumpur   Madrid   Melbourne   Mexico City
Mumbai   Nairobi   Paris   Singapore
Taipei   Tokyo   Toronto
and associates in
Berlin   Ibadan

Typeset by Rastrixi, New Delhi 110070
Printed in India at Rekha Printers Pvt. Ltd., New Delhi 110020
and published by Manzar Khan, Oxford University Press
YMCA Library Building, Jai Singh Road, New Delhi 110001

To the memory of
A. K. Ramanujan (1929–1993)
and
for the other poets and translators
in this book

A poet should learn with his eyes
the forms of leaves
he should know how to make
people laugh when they are together
he should get to see
what they are really like
he should know about oceans and mountains
in themselves
and the sun and the moon and the stars
his mind should enter into the seasons
he should go
among many people
in many places
and learn their languages

Kshemendra, *Kavikanthabharana*,
verses 10–11 (12th century);
translated from Sanskrit by
W.S. Merwin and J. Mousaieff-Mason

Acknowledgements

We would like to thank the poets and translators in this anthology for their help in preparing the final versions of the poems; and also Aparna Dharwadker, Emily Grosholz, Girish Karnad, and C.M. Naim, for reading earlier drafts and making valuable suggestions. We are particularly grateful to Arlene Zide for collecting new material by Indian women poets, and offering us some of her collaborative translations.

We are grateful to the Joint Committee on South Asia (Bernard S. Cohn, Chairman) of the American Council of Learned Societies and the Social Science Research Council, for timely summer funding; to the Department of South Asian Languages and Civilizations (C.M. Naim, Chairman) and the Committee on Social Thought (Paul Wheatley, Chairman), University of Chicago, for providing an ideal environment for the project, and facilities for endless manuscript preparation; to the Department of English, University of Georgia, and the Department of English, University of Oklahoma, for support in the final stages of the work. Thanks finally to James Nye, Bibliographer for South Asia, Regenstein Library, University of Chicago, for help with information on some of the poets; and to Michelle Stie, research assistant, University of Oklahoma, for help with correspondence and indexing.

Preface

This is an anthology of poems and translations. Translations, and anthologies of the kind we are offering here, are attempts at transmission—and more than transmission. For when they succeed, as Yehuda Amichai says,

> quietly we tra:.sfer words from man to man,
> from one tongue to other lips,
> and not knowingly, like a father
> who transfers the features of his dead father's face
> to his son,
> and himself doesn't look like either.

If they succeed, they change emphases, attack old biases and introduce new ones, even remake (ever so slightly, in a famous phrase) a reader's sense of his or her literary tradition.

Like other anthologies, this one carries the shape of its editors' obsessions and tastes. When the two of us met in Chicago several years ago, we found that we shared an addiction to translation, a constant curiosity about what was being written in all our Indian languages, and an unhappy impatience with most translated contemporary poems from India. Across two generations and different languages, we also discovered that we wanted to edit the same kind of anthology—one that would question and change many common assumptions about modern Indian poetry.

When we began work on this selection, we decided to limit ourselves to single poems which had reached both of us effectively through English. Over the next five years, independently and together, we searched for good poems we considered readably translated. We did not ask if a poem we liked was 'the best' or 'the most representative' of a poet, a style, a movement, or a language. We only asked ourselves whether the poem we saw through the translation looked good, whether it touched us even in translation and satisfied our needs and standards as long-term readers of Indian and English poetry.

Our search, however, was neither innocent nor arbitrary.

As we sifted systematically through about five thousand modern Indian poems translated from twenty languages, we kept going back to poems and poets we had known for a long time. We looked especially hard at the translations of poets who have reputations as twentieth-century Indian writers of the first importance. We did not let reputations dictate our choices, but we also did not take them lightly. As we went back and forth between different opinions, we found ourselves accumulating a few dozen poems which stood firmly on their own in their English versions, and at the same time represented something larger and richer in the Indian languages. We then added other poems, poets, and languages, and tried out various arrangements, in order to give the selection a measure of balance. What we settled for in the end was a group of one hundred and twenty-five poems by one hundred and twenty-five poets, arranged in an interacting thematic sequence. These poems represent—at least for now—the tentative positive findings of our search.

To reach this stage, we rummaged and rifled, often despairingly, through the innumerable catalogued and uncatalogued Indian books and periodicals on the shelves of the Joseph Regenstein Library at the University of Chicago. We pestered colleagues who knew other languages to give us lists of favourites, if not actual poems. We leafed through magazines like *The Illustrated Weekly of India* and *Quest*, not to mention the sexy centre-spreads of *Debonair*. We browsed through old anthologies and looked for new manuscripts in the mail. When we found a poem or translation one of us liked, we went over it together. Often we thought of changes which would make the poem sound better to our ears or look cleaner on the page. In the languages we knew—Kannada, Tamil, Hindi, Marathi—we frequently went back to the originals and made alternative versions. We then offered our suggestions to the original translators for checking and approval, and for any further changes these might trigger. As the reader will soon discover, the most satisfying translations often came from Indian-English poets, who bring to a native sense of their mother tongues a sensibility trained in the traditions of English writing.

Not all the poems here are translations. We have included

twenty Indian-English poems in our selection, which are as much a part of modern Indian poetry as the one hundred and five poems offered in translation. The translations themselves come from fourteen languages: Assamese, Bengali, Dogri, Gujarati, Hindi, Kannada, Malayalam, Marathi, Oriya, Punjabi, Sindhi, Tamil, Telugu, and Urdu. We have given these languages different amounts of space, depending on the quality of the material we found in each case. For some languages, especially those we know well, we have chosen between fourteen and sixteen poems in each (Bengali, Hindi, Kannada, Marathi). For the rest, we have selected between five and ten poems each in some cases (Gujarati, Malayalam, Oriya, Tamil, Telugu, Urdu), and less than five poems in others (Assamese, Dogri, Punjabi, Sindhi). Grouped together differently, the translations include exactly seventy poems from the ten Indo-Aryan languages on our list, and thirty-five poems from the four Dravidian languages. The amount of space given to a particular language, style, movement, region, or poet does not necessarily reflect on its (or his or her) position in the overall picture of modern Indian poetry. At the same time, our emphases are not accidents, and should also indicate our own preferences.

The one hundred and five translations are the work of sixty-seven individual translators, including more than a dozen important women translators. Most of the translators are Indian, but a few are British, European, or North American, some of them poets in their own right. These men and women usually work alone, sometimes with unexpected languages and in unsuspected places. But several of them also collaborate with each other, often over long periods of time, adding patiently to our store of translated poetry. In fact, the range of people and preoccupations involved in the translation of modern Indian poetry is, for us, one of the happy discoveries of this volume.

Taken as a group, the translations suggest what has been going on in the Indian translator's world in recent times. Approximately thirty of the versions we have chosen have appeared in earlier anthologies of modern Indian poetry, or in individual translated collections. But nearly fifty of the translations have been published in Indian, American, Canadian, and British magazines in the last fifteen years, many of them in the late

1980s, and about twenty-five translations are drawn from manuscripts still awaiting publication. These figures indicate that in the last two decades new translators and new translations have begun changing the situation of modern Indian poetry, reaching out at once to new material and to new audiences. We have tried to keep pace with these developments, and especially to select the best of what is available now—in several cases, from languages that were simply not translated extensively or well enough even twenty years ago.

Although we have omitted many prominent and famous names, the one hundred and twenty-five poets in these pages are among the best known in their respective languages. As a group, they are extremely diverse and serve as a good sample of the modern Indian literary world. Not only do they come from a wide variety of linguistic, regional, social, professional, economic, political, and even religious backgrounds, but collectively they also cover many of the important schools and movements in twentieth-century Indian poetry. (Some of the historical, social, and literary contexts of the work represented here are discussed in the Afterword.) The oldest writer in this book was born in the early 1860s, while the youngest was born nearly a century later. Within the span of the twentieth century, we have highlighted a number of poets who established their reputations before the end of the British Raj. But, at the same time, we have also emphasized the work of a large number of post-colonial poets, including a sizeable group of thirty-two women writers (drawn from thirteen languages), and at least half a dozen writers from traditionally marginalized positions in Indian society.

Similarly, the poems we have chosen also indicate the variety which we find in modern Indian poetry as a whole. The earliest poem here was written in the mid-1910s, while the latest was written about seventy-five years later, at the end of the 1980s. Between these two points, our selection ranges over most of the important types of verse Indian poets have produced in the twentieth century. Thus, in spite of its highly selective nature, our anthology has the scope and variety to make it a small but useful guide to the crowded landscape of modern Indian poetry.

But even as we say this, we would like to stress that what we have begun here is an *open* anthology, a selection in which we have implicitly raised questions even while committing ourselves to explicit choices. By the word 'open' we express a hope: that our choices will be weighed and probed, opening up concrete new discussions of what is valuable in Indian poetry today. We hope that this book will stir readers to suggest and offer other poems, poets, and translations, so that we (or others) may re-think, rearrange, and revise our present selection. If our fellow-readers find many of our choices as good as we think they are, if the majority of poems in these pages adds something readable and memorable to our meagre stock of what is readable and memorable in translations of modern Indian poetry, then we will have succeeded in doing what we set out to do. We have a distant hope that, in time, most of these poems will find their way to schools, textbooks, and young readers, enlarging our view, our repertoire, even our 'pantheon', of what we consider Indian.

This small anthology, we promise (knowing full well that in every promise is a threat), is only a beginning. Anthologies, as we began by saying, are opportunities: opportunities to sift, revaluate, rethink ourselves and our traditions; or simply to assert our tastes, laying them on the line in the service of discussion, in 'the common pursuit of true judgement', however elusive and conflict-ridden these may be.

Chicago,   Vinay Dharwadker and A.K. Ramanujan
September 1991

Postscript

To the deep regret of his family and friends, as well as readers and admirers around the world, A.K. Ramanujan passed away due to an irreversible heart disturbance during minor surgery in Chicago on Tuesday, 13 July 1993. His death was untimely: in the last few years he was at the height of his powers, writing new poems and essays, learning new languages, collecting and translating large quantities of uncollected and untranslated Indian material, and influencing a fresh generation of students and scholars. One of my own deepest regrets is, and will continue to be, that he did not see this book in print. Over the past three decades he had frequently imagined a well-crafted anthology of this kind, which would place the best twentieth-century Indian poems, in the best available translations, before the international readership they deserve. In the final years of his life he was particularly excited by the fact that, in our slow but successful collaboration, he and I had begun to translate his vision into practice. In retrospect I am happy that he revised the manuscript once more as late as 1992, adding to it his own and others' most recent versions of poems by several young men and women poets.

In 1988, while this book was still in draft form, Ramanujan and I had agreed to dedicate the project to the nearly two hundred poets, translators, and colleagues whose work made it possible in the first place. It is tragic, but wholly appropriate, that I should now dedicate it especially to his memory, even while retaining the original dedication. I cannot help but notice that Kshemendra's twelfth-century Sanskrit verse, as translated by W.S. Merwin and J. Mousaieff-Mason, which we together chose as the epigraph to the anthology, now seems to be two things at once: a prescription for an ideal poet, and a perfect description of Ramanujan himself.

Norman, Oklahoma   Vinay Dharwadker
4 February 1994

Contents

I. On Reading a Love Poem

P.S. Rege (1910–78)

The Pact

There were two conditions
to the pact—
there were two conditions to the pact
she and I made.
First: she could break it at any time.
Second: I could never break it.
We took our vows
with the echo in the hills as our witness,
made a bed of the wind,
and drew the sheet of the stars over ourselves—
and there was more, much more.
But so far
she hasn't kept her side of the bargain.
What should I do now with the second condition?
Is a pact merely a pact?

Translated from Marathi by Vinay Dharwadker

N. Revathi Devi (1951–81)

This Night

If this night passes
which does not surrender even to sleeping pills
if this night passes

the night that spreads under my back
like a bed of arrows
for not compromising with man

the night that flows in my veins
like blood from the thorns of the toddy palm
for not compromising with God
if this night passes

covering the face of honesty
with a blanket of light
another day
another day another night another day

at some time another night another day
if honesty stands naked, smooth
not finding light
if that night stands without passing
it will pass, it will move away, honestly

Translated from Telugu by V. Narayana Rao
and A.K. Ramanujan

Kedarnath Singh (*b.* 1934)

On Reading a Love Poem

When I'd read that long love poem
I closed the book and asked—
Where are the ducks?

I was surprised that they were nowhere
even far into the distance

It was in the third line of the poem
or perhaps the fifth
that I first felt
there might be ducks here somewhere

I'd heard the flap flap of their wings
but that may have been my illusion

I don't know for how long
that woman
had been standing in the twelfth line
waiting for a bus

The poem was completely silent
about where she wanted to go
only a little sunshine
sifted from the seventeenth line
was falling on her shoulders

The woman was happy
at least there was nothing in her face to suggest
that by the time she reached the twenty-first line
she'd disappear completely
like every other woman

There were *sakhu* trees
standing where the next line began
the trees were spreading
a strange dread through the poem

Every line that came next
was a deep disturbing fear and doubt
about every subsequent line

If only I'd remembered—
it was in the nineteenth line
that the woman was slicing potatoes

She was slicing
large round brown potatoes
inside the poem
and the poem was becoming
more and more silent
more solid

I think it was the smell
of freshly chopped vegetables
that kept the woman alive
for the next several lines

By the time I got to the twenty-second line
I felt that the poem was changing its location
like a speeding bullet
the poem had whizzed over the woman's shoulder
towards the *sakhu* trees

There were no lines after that
there were no more words in the poem
there was only the woman
there were only
her shoulders her back
her voice—
there was only the woman
standing whole outside the poem now
and breaking it to pieces

Translated from Hindi by Vinay Dharwadker

P. Lankesh (*b.* 1935)

Mother

My mother,
black, prolific earth mother,
a green leaf, a festival of white flowers;
earthier with every burn,
with every pang
more fruit and petal;
her limbs thrilled to children's kicks:
laying down the basket on her head,
she groaned, closed her eyes, never opened them again.

She raised a hundred measures of millet
to please my father
and win a bracelet for her arm;
swilling water for each clod of earth,
for pepper, pea, millet and grain,

she ploughed with her hand:
blossoming in flowers, ripening in fruit,
she watched over the fields,
spending her youth in a tatter of saris.

She died, she did:
what's the age of a hag bent double?
How many new year moons,
how many festivals of sugar bread
over the live coals? How many times
had she wept, this woman,
for coin, for dead calf, for ruined grain?
How many times had she roamed the villages
for some ancient runaway buffalo?

No, she was no Savitri,
no Sita or Urmila,
no heroine out of history books,
tranquil, fair and grave in dignity;
nor like the wives of Gandhi and Ramakrishna.
She didn't worship the gods
or listen to holy legends;
she didn't even wear, like a good wife,
any vermilion on her brow.

A wild bear
bearing a litter of little ones,
she reared a husband, saved coins in a knot of cloth;
like a hurt bitch, she bared her teeth,
growled and fought.
She was mean, crooked, ready to scratch like a monkey;
her only rule: whatever raises a family.
She would burn and flare
if a son went wild, or the husband elsewhere.

A jungle bear has no need for your Gita.
My mother lived
for stick and grain, labour and babies;
for a rafter over her head,
rice, bread, a blanket;
to walk upright among equals.

Admiration, tears, thanks:
for bearing and raising us;
for living in mud and soil, for leaving as she did,
as if leaving home for the fields,
cool as usual,
in the middle of small talk.

Translated from Kannada by A.K. Ramanujan

Gagan Gill (*b.* 1959)

The Girl's Desire Moves Among Her Bangles

The girl's desire moves among her bangles
They should break first on his bed
Then on the threshold of his house.

But why on the threshold?

Because a woman sits grieving inside the girl
A woman who's a widow
No, not really one
But a woman who'll surely become
A widow.

The girl's fear throbs in her veins
And moves across her bangles
The girl's desire throbs in her bangles
And they throb with her sorrow.

Sorrow?

Where's this girl's man?
The man who's in her mourning veins
Who fills her bangles with desire?

Her man lies caught
In someone else's body
Someone else's dream, someone else's sorrow
Someone else's tears
Each one of his sorrows, dreams, tears
Lies beyond the girl's mourning grasp.

But the girl's still a girl
The same primitive innocence in her
Fills her with madness, a deathwish
For which she will always punish the man
In the days to come.
When she will smash her bangles
On the threshold of his house. . . .

Translated from Hindi by Mrinal Pande and Arlene Zide

Rabindranath Tagore (1861–1941)

Flute-music

Kinu the milkman's alley.
   A ground-floor room in a two-storeyed house,
Slap on the road, windows barred.
   Decaying walls, crumbling to dust in places
     Or stained with damp.
     Stuck on the door,
   A picture of Ganesha, Bringer of Success,
     From the end of a bale of cloth.
Another creature apart from me lives in my room
     For the same rent:
       A lizard.

There's one difference between him and me:
He doesn't go hungry.
I get twenty-five rupees a month
As junior clerk in a trading office.
I'm fed at the Dattas' house
For coaching their boy.
At dusk I go to Sealdah station,
Spend the evening there
To save the cost of light.
Engines chuffing,
Whistles shrieking,
Passengers scurrying,
Coolies shouting.
I stay till half past ten,
Then back to my dark, silent, lonely room.

A village on the Dhaleshvari river, that's where my aunt's
people live.
Her brother-in-law's daughter—
She was due to marry my unfortunate self, everything was
fixed.
The moment was indeed auspicious for her, no doubt of
that—
For I ran away.
The girl was saved from me,
And I from her.
She did not come to this room,
but she's in and out of my mind all the time:
Dacca sari, vermilion on her forehead.

Pouring rain.
My tram costs go up,
But often as not my pay gets cut for lateness.
Along the alley,
Mango skins and stones, jack-fruit pulp,
Fish-gills, dead kittens
And God knows what other rubbish
Pile up and rot.
My umbrella is like my depleted pay—
Full of holes.

My sopping office clothes ooze
    Like a pious Vaishnava.
      Monsoon darkness
    Sticks in my damp room
    Like an animal caught in a trap,
      Lifeless and numb.
Day and night I feel strapped bodily
    On to a half-dead world.

    At the corner of the alley lives Kantababu—
      Long hair carefully parted,
        Large eyes,
          Cultivated tastes.
      He fancies himself on the cornet:
    The sound of it comes in gusts
      On the foul breeze of the alley—
Sometimes in the middle of the night,
    Sometimes in the early morning twilight,
      Sometimes in the afternoon
    When sun and shadows glitter.
      Suddenly this evening
He starts to play runs in Sindhu-Baroya raga,
    And the whole sky rings
    With eternal pangs of separation.
    At once the alley is a lie,
False and vile as the ravings of a drunkard,
And I feel that nothing distinguishes Haripada the clerk
    From the Emperor Akbar.
Torn umbrella and royal parasol merge,
    Rise on the sad music of a flute
      Towards one heaven.

    The music is true
Where, in the everlasting twilight of my wedding,
    The Dhaleshvari river flows,
    Its banks deeply shaded by *tamal*-trees,
And she who waits in the courtyard
Is dressed in a Dacca sari, vermilion on her forehead.

Translated from Bengali by William Radice

Eunice de Souza (*b.* 1940)

Women in Dutch Painting

The afternoon sun is on their faces.
They are calm, not stupid,
pregnant, not bovine.
I know women like that
and not just in paintings—
an aunt who did not answer her husband back,
not because she was plain,
and an aunt who writes poems
and hopes her avocado seeds
will sprout in the kitchen.
Her voice is oatmeal and honey.

Aziz Qaisi (*b.* 1945)

Outside the Furnace

Every day
she threw her supple arms,
her soft, silken thighs,
her round young breasts,
her rosy lips and cheeks,
her glossy black hair,
and all her body parts
into the burning furnace.
A thick liquid,
the colour of silver and gold,
congealed and set
in the hot and cold forms of her breaths
and became her body.

One night
when she threw her body
into the burning furnace,
the gold and silver liquid would not set
in the hot and cold forms of her breaths.
All her limbs were scattered.
First her lips,
then her cheeks,
and then her arms were thrown apart.
Her hair was scorched,
her breasts were consumed,
her waist was seared,
her thighs were parched.
Then the heavy liquid,
turning into jagged golden nuggets,
sank into her bones
until she died.

But her eyes still live.
They say to me:
Throw your body's steel,
the glass of your heart
into the furnace.
Look, every day and every night and every moment,
you too are dying, just like me.
Everyone is dying, just like me.
But take this warning
and save your eyes.

Translated from Urdu by Baidar Bakht and Leslie Lavigne

Vinda Karandikar (*b.* 1918)

The Knot

> Balancing
> its weight on the horizon's balustrade
> for a moment, the leukaemic evening
> disappeared into the hospital in the west.
> The fronds
> of the coconut palm behind the public bench
> were shivering at the wind's touch.
> She said,
> 'Eight years ago the green fronds
> of this tree used to brush against our backs.
> You remember, don't you?'
> He remembered
> how he'd started when the fronds had touched
> his back while he was kissing her passionately,
> how suddenly a fear had shaken him—
> like the abominable snowman wandering
> on the edge of the mind's precipice—
> 'Yes, I remember,'
> he said—'Have you noticed how many
> coconuts there are on this small palm?'
> He didn't realize it,
> but his words touched her sense of inadequacy
> without meaning to. She drew the end
> of her sari around herself and hugged
> the plastic purse close to her flat chest.
> 'Can I ask you something?'
> she said—'How long are we going
> to keep meeting each other like this?'
> He fidgeted with the finger he was holding
> in Sartre's *God and Satan* to mark a page
> and muttered, 'Who knows?'
> A little troubled, confused, crestfallen.

              Irritated,
she said, 'You! You ought to know!'
The certainty with which he had known things
eight years ago had dissolved
in the cesspool of his circumstances.
He remembered the great critique of the War
he'd composed; the expectations
he'd built up; the castles he'd built
on the future's mist—now all crumbling.
          A parade celebrating the fourth
          anniversary of the end of the War
          was passing down the street in front of them,
          cheering the reign of peace in its voice of steel.
              Just then
he was struck by an earlier memory—
another girl—another ruptured moment—
those days, premature, twisted out of shape,
running around in circles round the fire.
Their endless wealth of anguish,
now lost. 'No! Impossible!' he said to himself,
laughing at his own dead self.
'I couldn't have done it! But if I had—
if I had—if only I were man enough!'
He muttered, 'What's bound to happen, happens.'
The late April sun had beaded
the two furrows on his brow with sweat.
              'You know,'
she said, 'You ought to know,'
in a provocative tone. (In other words,
a tone of voice she'd learnt by heart
while going around with Eknath Samant.
—If Eknath hadn't won himself
a permanent commission—then maybe—
but why—the lousy bastard!)
              'You know,'
she said, 'You know. It seems you've forgotten—
"When the War has ended," you'd said.'
              'Yes, I'd said it.
When my health has improved a little,

When my life has become stable.'
                    Playing with her buttons,
she pretended that she wasn't angry,
and muttered something inaudible.
She was really very tired; very weary;
that's why it wasn't going to do her any good
to be so impatient now.
            Now there were workers
            marching towards a factory
            shouting, 'Long Live the Revolution!'
            and demanding two months' extra pay as a bonus.
                    She spluttered,
'Tell me once and for all—
when will your great war end?'
                    He said,
'Who knows, who knows'—
'Go ask that madman there,'
she said with amazing sarcasm.
—Across the street a local idiot
was walking around with rags
bundled up on his head, looking for more.
                    He thought,
we're both trapped in a huge wheel—
we're stuck in it—and it's hurtling down
the steep slope of time,
without direction, without will—
in that great headlong plunge of destiny
he saw the freedom of his own desire,
like a whirlpool—the desire to know,
not to live; to choose, not to act.
                    In that moment of clarity
he drew the retrenchment notice
from his plastic wallet—he'd received it
earlier that day—and placed the piece of paper,
this paper sob, in her hand—the hand
with which she was playing with a button.
                    That day
she went away with the resolve
never to come back again. In her heart,

she drew strength from her shattered hopes;
when she saw the future's skeleton,
her fear of uncertainty melted away.
That day for the first time she found
strength in loneliness. She found the courage
that comes from hopelessness.
         And he too
found a little unexpected satisfaction
when she turned her back to him—
for the first time in eight years
he saw in her braided hair
the knot of a braid of artificial hair.

Translated from Marathi by Vinay Dharwadker

A.K. Ramanujan (1929–93)

Love Poem for a Wife, 2

After a night of rage
that lasted days,
quarrels in a forest,
waterfalls, exchanges, marriage,
exploration of bays
and places
we had never known
we would ever know,

my wife's always
changing syriac face,
chosen of all faces,
a pouting difficult child's
changing in the chameleon
emerald
wilderness of Kerala,
small cousin to tall

mythic men, rubber plant
and peppervine,
frocks with print patterns
copied locally
from the dotted
butterfly,
grandmother wearing white
day and night in a village

full of the colour schemes
of kraits and gartersnakes;
adolescent in Aden among stabbing
Arabs, betrayed and whipped
yet happy among ships
in harbour,
and the evacuees,
the borrowed earth

under the borrowed trees;
taught dry and wet,
hot and cold
by the monsoon then,
by the siroccos now
on copper
dustcones, the crater
townships in the volcanoes

of Aden:
                    I dreamed one day
that face my own yet hers,
with my own nowhere
to be found; lost; cut

loose like my dragnet
past.
I woke up and groped,
turned on the realism

of the ceiling light,
found half a mirror
in the mountain cabin
fallen behind the dresser
to look at my face now
and the face
of her sleep, still asleep
and very syriac on the bed

behind: happy for once
at such loss of face,
whole in the ambivalence
of being halfwoman half-
man contained in a common
body,
androgynous as a god
balancing stillness in the middle

of a duel to make it dance:
soon to be myself, a man
unhappy in the morning
to be himself again,
the past still there,
a drying
net on the mountain,

in the morning, in the waking
my wife's face still fast
asleep, blessed as by
butterfly, snake, shiprope,
and grandmother's other
children,
by my only love's only
insatiable envy.

Jyotsna Milan (*b.* 1941)

Woman, 2

Sometimes
in the moments of lovemaking
the man seems God-like to the woman.
'God . . . God!' the woman calls out,
her body
set on fire.
'Look,'
the man says,
'I'm God.'
The woman
looks,
and convulsing with the pain
of losing God,
she turns away
her face.

Translated from Hindi by Mrinal Pande
and Arlene Zide

II.   A Pond Named Ganga

K.S. Narasimhaswami (*b.* 1915)

Consolation to Empty Pitchers

In the heat of noon
the waterless watertap
offers consolation
to empty pitchers.
There's not a face in the street.
It's all occupied by the sun.

The sky is one unending blue,
with no luck
and no breath left.

You can talk about night
to the night, but what about now?
Not one white cloud.
Beyond the town, beyond the respiration
of a million lives,
in someone's desert field,
the smalltown herds of cattle
bend their heads,
grazing
on burntout weeds and tares.

A minute ago
the cowbells chimed
over the fences.
A column of smoke rises now
in front of the boulder,
from dry leaves in the fire
of no desire.

At the temple door, chimeras,
the sun's horses,
pass in silence: no pearls
on them, no god to ride them,
they neither kick nor bite,
these nominal horses!

Who needs these processions
of dead glory?

Weary, lame, the mind
finds a mudhouse a mountain.
A lorry gasps in a cloud of dust.
Why does the plane in the sky
look so slow?
A threadless needle
stuck in a blue cloth.
The trees are dishevelled, tinder-dry,
in the sun.

Beauty's eye the colour of dust,
thirst burns small
in the mouth of poetry.
This is hell, with no touch of green,
wet mud, or wisp of breath.
This old tree is a hollow bole,
no bird will alight on it,
no monkey hang from it.
What's the point of this deathlessness?
Gone dry, sucking for a century
on springs, its body is a nest
only for vipers.
Who needs it?
I wish a storm would blow it down.

What did you say was the colour
of beauty's eye? what burns small
in poetry's mouth?
It's written in the old book:
a full vessel is still.
(Good writing.)
Tomorrow in a thousand streets
there will be a procession of the goddess,
Ganga, goddess of waters.

The waterless tap
softly softly consoles
empty pitchers:

a full vessel is still,
it doesn't slosh,
ever.
But then,
neither does an empty one.
Never mind sloshing, where where
where is the water?

No answer.
Waterless, the watertap
murmurs consolations
to empty pitchers:
a full vessel is still,
it doesn't slosh,
ever.

Translated from Kannada by A.K. Ramanujan

B.S. Mardhekar (1909–56)

The Forest of Yellow Bamboo Trees

The forest of yellow bamboo trees
underlines the sky with its song;
between the lines, the mind grinds up
the promise to live (not now, but tomorrow).

The lemon tree carves in the wind
old neuter futures horned with antlers;
and footprints are printed on that wind,
but they're dead, though new.

Countless crows splotch their lime
on the pylons of the centuries;
and verbs stand guard round the clock,
but though they're alert, they're robots.

The polestar that never sets has set,
the Seven Sages have botched their answer;
hail that's not yet frozen falls,
and on the radio, Radha and Krishna.

Translated from Marathi by Vinay Dharwadker

Nissim Ezekiel (*b.* 1924)

from *Hymns in Darkness*

7

There's only this:
            a tarred road
            under a mild sun
            after rain,
            glowing;

            wet, green leaves
            patterned flat
            on the pavement
            around dog-shit;

            one ragged slipper
            near an open gutter,
            three crows
            pecking away at it.

And breasts, thighs, buttocks
            swinging
            now towards
            now away from him.

11

The Enemy is God
as the Unchanging One.

All forms of God
and the God in all forms.

The absentee landlord,
the official of all officials.

The oppressor who worships God
and the oppressed who worship God

are victims of the Enemy.
They rot in families, in castes,

in communities, in clubs,
in political parties.

They stay stable. They stay still.
Their hands continue to keep down the young.

13

I met a man once
who had wasted half his life,

partly in exile from himself,
partly in a prison of his own making.

An energetic man, an active man.
I liked his spirit
and saw no hope for him.

Yet, he had the common touch;
he could, for instance, work with his hands.

To others, all attentive.
To his own needs, indifferent.

A tireless social human being,
destined always
to know defeat
like a twin-brother.

I saw him cheerful
in the universal darkness
as I stood grimly
in my little light.

14

He said:
'In a single day
I'm forced to listen
to a dozen film songs,
to see
a score of beggars,
to touch
uncounted strangers,
to smell
unsmellable smells,
to taste
my bitter native city.'

He said:
'I'm forced by the five senses
to fear the five senses.'

I heard him out
in black wordlessness.

G.M. Muktibodh (1917–64)

The Void

The void inside us
has jaws,
those jaws have carnivorous teeth;
those teeth will chew you up,
those teeth will chew up everyone else.
The dearth inside
is our nature,
habitually angry,
in the dark hollow inside the jaws
there is a pond of blood.
This void is utterly black,
is barbaric, is naked,
disowned, debased,
completely self-absorbed.
I scatter it,
give it away,
with fiery words and deeds.
Those who cross my path
find this void
in the wounds
I inflict on them.
They let it grow,
spread it around,
scatter it and give it away
to others,
raising the children of emptiness.
The void is very durable,
it is fertile.
Everywhere it breeds
saws, daggers, sickles,
breeds carnivorous teeth.
That is why,
wherever you look,

there is dancing, jubilation,
death is now giving birth
to brand new children.
Everywhere
there are oversights
with the teeth of saws,
there are heavily armed mistakes:
the world looks at them
and walks on,
rubbing its hands.

Translated from Hindi by Vinay Dharwadker

Hira Bansode (*b.* 1939)

Woman

She, the river,
said to him, the sea:
    All my life
    I've been dissolving myself
    and flowing towards you
    for your sake
    in the end it was I
    who turned into the sea
    a woman's gift
    is as large as the sky
        but you went on
        worshipping yourself
        you never thought
        of becoming a river
        and merging
        with me

Translated from Marathi by Vinay Dharwadker

Archana Varma (*b.* 1946)

Man

Water on a slope
will run downhill, they said
with an air of finality.
That is, if water is water.

They didn't say that soil on a slope
if it's really soil
will soak up water.
That a green carpet of grass
will sprout, covering the slope.
It may lie covering the slope
but it will turn its face skywards.
That is, if grass is really grass.

We're all standing on a slope.
This was the topic of discussion
that evening. Water
can only flow downwards.
This was their conclusion.
Trees were not discussed at all.
They may spring up
at the bottom of the slope
but they grow upwards.
The bigger they grow
the easier they're uprooted.
That is, if trees are really trees.

But the water
wasn't water. And the grass
wasn't grass either. Or the trees,
trees. But the topic
wasn't water, or grass, or trees.
It was man, and about him
no one said a word.

Translated from Hindi by Aruna Sitesh and Arlene Zide

Ismail (*b.* 1928)

The Wall

I know
what should be out
and what should be in.
But then
what's this window doing here?

Translated from Telugu by V. Narayana Rao

Munib-ur-Rahman (*b.* 1924)

Tall Buildings

All our lives
we crawled in the shadow
of tall buildings,
clinging to the walls.
The buildings were tall mountains
and we were ants,
always in search of food.
Tall buildings loomed in the way
whenever friends came together.
These buildings grew and grew
even as we shrank.
At last, one day, we disappeared,
leaving behind
nothing but tall buildings.

Translated from Urdu by Kathleen Grant Jaeger
and Baidar Bakht

Vijaya Mukhopadhyay (*b.* 1937)

Monday

At the crack of dawn, Monday stands beside you,
　　　　　his hand on your shoulder.
Soon, people start moving about;
sweat, fragrance, and the inimitable noise of traffic
get mixed up, as if he had no hand in it.
His shirt is mauve
on moss-green corduroy trousers;
his eyes are silent, determined,
　　　　　dimmed by a little shadow.
Whenever I say something critical,
he raises a finger to his lips;
then slowly, under his finger's pressure,
his lips grow bigger and bigger,
until his mouth is like a red clay drum,
　　　　　a pomegranate's pod split open.
Pretending to pick burrs from his trousers,
I bend down and say—
We wander about busily like pygmies
on this planet controlled by satellites,
with no work, no reason to panic.
Monday, you're our passport
to the big wide world, our impetus—
　　　　　but even before I finish,
darkness bursts out of the basement
and he vanishes without a trace.

Translated from Bengali by Sunil B. Ray,
Carolyne Wright, and the poet

Jayanta Mahapatra (b. 1928)

An October Morning

Dawn edges its way through the crowd of huddled trees,
a mole scurries away behind a fallen log. Somewhere
the sound of a truck starting, like the question
one had sullenly fallen asleep with, resuming
in the brain. A flight of parakeets
circling for a while before their cries are lost
in the distance that holds the sunken river,
stoically silent. Cries that fill and empty the mind
at the same time, touching the decaying timber
by the shore, a trail losing itself in life,
saying nothing. How do we know what we are like, when we
can turn to the dreams we find, and build
the pose of distance to serve as a symbol?
And what a lone cry does sometimes, heading through
to the empty room where man can dream up ways
to prey on his own kind? Thinner than this dawn light
are the instants inside of us that reach the top
of the rise, where the world spreads the slow flush
of beginning once again, and where we clearly forget
our own deaths. A breathless light in which a woman
suddenly realizes that she must find something
to hide her nakedness. And in which a temple too
can send its sleepy bells fluttering
over the smug roofs like a flock of pigeons.
The morning is here, looking out of a hole
in a clay bank like the furry snout of a jackal,
as familiar dark-eyed women shout to one another
near the public water faucet; and two boys,
sensing their parents' wrongs, grow up genially to be men;
and we know we aren't ready for answers or for the heart's
cries, as a web of light is flung across those dim places
of the body where we hate to hide again.

Padma Sachdev (*b*. 1940)

The Well

To the right
of our hill
there's a shining well
full of water.
Last year
summer covered it
with green mango blossom.
The green tempted
a calf,
which fell in
and drowned.
Since then
people have stopped
drinking from that well.
Now, like a thief,
I bathe in it
at night.
I cup my hands
and drink from it
at night.
But the water
doesn't quench
my thirst, my desire.
In the dark depths
of the well
there are shadows
still waiting for
the girls
who'd slung a rope
on its hook
but never came back
to draw water.

The well's darkness
is waiting
for the moment
when I'll have
the courage
to stretch out my hands
and drink its water
in broad daylight.

Translated from Dogri by Iqbal Masud

Sitanshu Yashashchandra (*b.* 1941)

Drought

For nearly a month
the tortoise has been lying there,
stony as an adam's apple.
Terraces, like the tongues of flaming caves,
lie empty at noon.
From the gaping doors,
black tar drips like thick saliva.

Mother told us
that after the tortoises
there would be fish in the well,
that we should watch it intently with the torch—
you can't let the well dry up in this terrible famine.
For who knows,
the wall of this mysterious cave
might open up,
and in the halo of this light
fish, crocodile, hippopotamus
and, what mother didn't know, even sea horses
might come flying from the wall
into the baffled eye of the torch.

Who knows who inscribed
a sea horse on this cave wall?
It has been there for years, decades, centuries,
flying in the water.
And in this terrible drought,
as the well goes on opening deeper
and deeper downwards,
the horses on the ghostly cave walls
begin to neigh bucketfuls,
and the sprightly cheetahs. . . .
Now you experience such a bottomless fear
when you're thirsty,
while tying the master-knot to let the rope down,
that you recall the story of Sadevant Savalinga,
in which the bewitching knot of night
suddenly undoes itself;
and as you haul wet rope over slippery pulley
bucketfuls of blind, upturned, twitching, gentle bats
come tumbling out of this dark, obscure,
hollow, phantom cave.

In this unforeseen time of drought
blank sky and fever-hot directionless space
slip away into the unfound routes of terraces.
In the deep recesses of the cave,
in this desolate noon,
the cheetahs and fish who have slept
for centuries might come awake in the wall.
The throat is parched and the mouth is burning with fever.
But one has lost the nerve to lower
another bucket into the well.
As tired hands let the rope slip
the bucket falls to the bottom.
And when the cat-hook is lowered to retrieve it,
the sprightly cheetahs hiss out in a pack.
You feel ashamed to turn the torch on them, and yet—
should you or shouldn't you pull up the cat-hook?
You wonder if in this unexpected season of drought
these iron cats of drag-hooks have given birth

to golden kittens in these dark hollows,
in the secret well of doubt.

Though the mud-plaster is cracked
and is peeling off in the dryness,
and the well is an awful place to inhabit,
what would you do if worms and insects
crawled out of the cracks?
Under the hot curved metal faucet,
water trickles into the bucket,
but it dries up after a few drops.
Who will daub and restore
this constantly cracking mud wall?
And yet—

What is thirst?
As if dragged from the throat at night,
it lay crumpled, a late-morning bedsheet,
on dust-coated brows;
thirst pushed itself into the nostrils;
raw thirst sat on parched lips,
this high thirst passed through,
forcing itself deep into the gullet,
then gushed out from the navel.
The water in the well must be exhausted by now
from creating mirages of tortoises and fish,
followed by whales and other ghosts.

And yet it is not.
I remember mother saying
that if this well went dry—
no, she really said that,
these are no folk tales about sea horses and cheetahs—
if this well went dry,
perhaps within a month in this terrible drought,
the inside, the wall, the bottom
will overflow with innumerable ants
and a wellful of ants will swell and spill over.
A million ants from the foundations of this house
will cover the rooms and yawning terraces like tongues,

and on slippery pulleys with long ropes hanging
     everywhere,
ants and ants and ants, ants and ants
and ants, ants, ants, and nothing but ants.

Translated from Gujarati by Saleem Peeradina, Jayant Parekh,
Rasik Shah, and Ghulam Mohammed Sheikh

R. Meenakshi (*b.* 1944)

If Hot Flowers Come to the Street

> Red cassia flowers
> are a forest fire,
> or so they say.
> It's an April event
> called a summer fire.
> Anarchy in green.
> An explosion of buds.
> Fire in the snow.
>
> On the head of Lord Shiva
> of the snow mountains
> there are red matted locks,
>   gleaming cassia flowers,
>   and the Ganga.
>
> In his red hand,
>   fire,
>   a small drum,
>   a deer.

And a snake at his throat.
That snake
won't strike the deer.
The fire in his hand
won't burn the Ganga.

But in our street
even flies
will swarm to hot flowers.

Translated from Tamil by Martha Ann Selby

Agha Shahid Ali (*b.* 1949)

Desert Landscape

Stringing red serrano peppers, crushing
cilantro seeds—just a few yards from where,
in 1693, a Jesuit priest
began to build a boat, bringing rumours
of water to an earth still forgetting

the sea it had lost over two hundred
million years ago—three white-haired women
in veils, their faces young, guard the desert
as it gives up its memories of water
(the fossils of vanished species) while miles

from them the sky opens its hands above
a city being brought to memory by rain:
as silver veins erupt over the peaks
and the mountains catch fire, the three women
can see across the veiled miles the streets turn

to streams, then rivers, the poor running from
one another into each other's arms;
can see the moon drown, its dimmed heart gone out
like a hungry child's; can see all that will come—
for two have turned towards the dawn, their eyes

holding children washed from their mother's arms,
and the third, her face against the dark sky
but her fingers slowly white, has let drop
her string of dried peppers and is bringing
the sea—a hollow fossil—to her ear.

Chandrashekhar Kambar (b. 1938)

A Pond Named Ganga

Our village pond named Mother Ganga
stands where the red hill meets the white.
On all three sides grow a million plants,
a seven-walled fort
no man can enter or get out of.
In there, the grunt, growl, and screech
of dogs, foxes, pigs, and parrots
and numberless other creatures.
Each has its share of wind, rain, light, bush,
green, fodder, fear, sleep, and sex.
The trees on the bank have swarms of bats
hanging upside down,
with their broken reflections in the water below.
Generations of flies, fleas, bugs of every kind
breed in endless motion,
in unbroken exchanges of give and take.
The water has nowhere to go.

No great waves rise and fall here
and no cold winds blow,
but the water rustles in the roots of old trees,
swirls in the village gutters,
and in the round white holes of the crabs.

Any time the east's old carbuncle breaks
and oozes blood and pus,
movement begins here:
babysnake ripples wake, break, roll about,
and the flocks of bats break up into lines,
form sixes and sevens,
circle on their wrinkled wings.

In the muddy mired water,
one-legged herons walk,
pecking and devouring the floating glistening fish.
People begin to come for the water:
to drink, to bathe in, to wash
their cattle's dung and urine,
to reach our god Birappa's feet,
to bathe our Black Mother Goddess,
to piss and shit,
to wet orthodox widows' weeds,
to get the brahmins' holy water,
for this, that, and the other.
The water spent this way
runs down the gutters of the village
and comes back to the pond.
This daily round of commerce
is its specialty.

This water too has its Ganges Hymns,
its Hundred Names, its Thousand Names,
its place-legends,
braided by the village brahmins
like their own tufts.
It's the grease from the Old God's matted hair,
it's the green shit from the sage's thighs,
it's Mother Ganga herself who has stayed here

to wash the dirt from her ears.
When she came,
she came with a dowry in her lap,
the holy germs from the mud and sand of her country,
the fear that ropes are snakes,
the magic mirror held up to seeing eyes.

The Mother's powers are miraculous.
A copper coin turns green
the moment you dip it in this water.
Burnish it, and she deludes you
with impressions of gold.
She's the one who gave the sorceress of Bengal
a pregnant woman's dead hand for a wand.
Three gulps of her water
gives barren women firm embryos.
She has taken whole schoolchildren,
bikes and all, into her maw.
And she is the one who possessed
the untouchable woman
and said in her voice, 'Yes, O Yes!'
when the padre claimed,
'This is the water on which Jesus walked.'

Its depth is the bottom of the bottomless depth,
world below netherworld below worlds below,
not mud and pebble.
Anyone who says it is,
will have worms swarming in his mouth.
Four or five of our townsmen got down there,
and slept (they say) with serpent princesses—
they're now gods in stone, stories in ballads,
and they get worshipped on full-moon and festival days.
People say, the glittering fish
that guzzle on pearls and diamonds
can't digest them, and so float dead.
So too, night and day,
people become one-legged herons,
and ooze like saliva from the herons' beaks.

It's now the place for bastard children, the Karnas,
and for the cowards who can't accept them.
This is true. There are such men,
who have no burials, no claim on funeral fires.
They float on the water for three days and nights,
and then our Mother Ganga opens her eyes.
Then the bodies of these men
go to the water-creatures,
their souls to the trees
to become hanging bats.
They join the Mother's private police force
and guard her pearls and diamonds.

It's true there's no evidence
for any of these claims
in the brahmins' books or the shepherds' songs.
But the brahmin did say so once
in a trance.

Translated from Kannada by A.K. Ramanujan

III. Household Fires

Anuradha Mahapatra (b. 1956)

Spell

> Under the easy glide of water
> lies more water, concealed within oneself,
> oneself, unconditional melancholy's magnet.
> With a magic spell she imprisons
> in the dead lamp's hollow
>   the blind muse of desire.
> Whichever way life flows, so floats
> the sacred banyan leaf.

Translated from Bengali by Jyotirmoy Dutta
and Carolyne Wright

Mrinal Pande (b. 1946)

Two Women Knitting

Rama says,
Rama says to Uma,
Oh my,
How time passes.
Ah me, says Uma.
Then both fall silent.

The two women go on casting stitches.
They skip stitches, slip the skipped stitches over,
Knit over purl,
Purl over knit.
After many intricate loops and cables,
Their dark secrets still lie locked inside them,
They've thrown the keys to their jewellery boxes into the
    lake.
Insert the keys, and the locks will bleed real blood.

Two women knit,
Clicking metal on metal,
Passers-by look up amazed at the sparks that fly.
Loneliness turns up at every other row
Of stitches in their patterns,
Even though they've worn each other's saris
And bathed each other's slippery infants,
Even though at this very moment
Their husbands lie asleep in the rooms upstairs,
Shaking them in their dreams.

Translated from Hindi by the poet and Arlene Zide

Indira Sant (*b.* 1914)

Household Fires

The daughter's job: without a murmur
to do the chores piling up around the house
until she leaves for work,
to pay her younger brother's fees,
to buy her sister ribbons,
to get her father's spectacles changed.
To take the others to the movies on holidays,
to keep back a little and hand over the rest
on payday.

The son's job: to get fresh savoury snacks
for the whole household to eat,
to bring back the clothes from the washerman,
to clean and put away the bicycle,
to sing out of key while packing his father's lunch
at the last minute,
to open the door sulkily
whenever someone comes home from the movies,
to wrinkle his brow
when he puts out his hand for money
and is asked instead: 'How much? For what?'

The younger daughter's job:
to savour the joys of shyness,
to shrink back minute by minute.
The younger son's job:
to choke all the while, grow up slowly
in states of wet and dry.

Four children learning in her fold,
her body drained by hardship,
what's left of her,
this mother and wife? A mass of tatters,
five tongues of flame
licking and licking at her on every side,
fanning the fire in her eyes
till her mind boils over,
gets burnt.

Translated from Marathi by Vinay Dharwadker

S. Usha (*b.* 1954)

To Mother

> Mother, don't, please don't,
> don't cut off the sunlight
> with your sari spread across the sky
> blanching life's green leaves.
>
> Don't say: You're seventeen already,
> don't flash your sari in the street,
> don't make eyes at passers-by,
> don't be a tomboy riding the winds.
>
> Don't play that tune again
> that your mother,
> her mother and her mother
> had played on the snake-charmer's flute
> into the ears of nitwits like me.

I'm just spreading my hood.
I'll sink my fangs into someone
and lose my venom.
Let go, make way.

Circumambulating the holy plant
in the yard, making *rangoli* designs
to see heaven, turning up dead
without light and air,
for god's sake, I can't do it.
Breaking out of the dam
you've built, swelling
in a thunderstorm,
roaring through the land,
let me live, very different
from you, Mother.
Let go, make way.

Translated from Kannada by A.K. Ramanujan

Shanmuga Subbiah (*b.* 1924)

Salutations

Yes! Oh yes!
Indeed I'm blessed!
By God's grace
I have two children.
It's rather strange,
But both
Are boys.
So?
I'm rheumatic,
My wife's consumptive.
The first boy,
Poor chap,

Is quite sickly.
The younger one,
So far,
Is okay.
But later on—
Who knows?
I'm a clerk.
Will this do?
Or would you like to have
More details?

Translated from Tamil by T.K. Doraiswamy

G.S. Shivarudrappa (*b.* 1926)

This Man

His cauldrons seethe.
In the nest of his heart
it ticks:
a wreckage of clocks.

A hundred carriages
shuttle night and day
on these rails.

These are the noises.
Then comes the silence.

Light and dark goad him
as they run.
The east in embers,
and night
as she unfurls her parasol
of a million holes, and that flood
of sighs we call the wind,
all these run over him
without pity, without end.

Circuses, movies, restaurants,
acrobatic shows,
cigarettes, cards, snake-charming
feats, poetry circles, and the high-falutin'
of endless talks,
all that feast of myth and legend:
these and such as these
are placebos for his pain.

From the cracks in his ceiling
the rains, the thoughts stream
and muddy the floors. Yet
green are the shoots of desire.

Despair
doesn't quite drown him.
He doesn't curse his gods
but bears like a patient pole
a lamp upon his head.
His silence, a small fire,
keeps a vigil
in corruption's wakes and fairs.

Translated from Kannada by A.K. Ramanujan

Nirendranath Chakrabarti (*b.* 1924)

Amalkanti

Amalkanti is a friend of mine,
we were together at school.
He often came late to class
and never knew his lessons.
When asked to conjugate a verb,
he looked out of the window
in such puzzlement
that we all felt sorry for him.

Some of us wanted to be teachers,
some doctors, some lawyers.
Amalkanti didn't want to be any of these.
He wanted to be sunlight—
the timid sunlight of late afternoon,
when it stops raining
and the crows call again,
the sunlight that clings like a smile
to the leaves of the *jaam* and the *jaamrul.*

Some of us have become teachers,
some doctors, some lawyers.
Amalkanti couldn't become sunlight.
He works in a poorly lit room
for a printer.
He drops in now and then to see me,
chats about this and that
over a cup of tea, then gets up to go.
I see him off at the door.

The one among us who's a teacher
could easily have become a doctor.
If the one who'd wanted to be a doctor
had become a lawyer,
it wouldn't have made much difference to him.
All of us got more or less what we wanted,
all except Amalkanti—
who used to think so much about sunlight
that he wanted to become sunlight.

Translated from Bengali by Sujit Mukherjee
and Meenakshi Mukherjee

Akhtar-ul-Iman (*b.* 1915)

Compromise

Whenever I kissed her,
the smell of cigarettes filled my nostrils.
I've always thought of smoking as a vice,
but now I'm used to it,
it's a part of me.
She too has got used to my stained teeth.
Whenever we meet, we become strangers to words,
only our breathing, sweat, and loneliness
fill the room.
Maybe our souls are dead,
our senses have run dry,
or this story's repeated over and over again:
life's always going through the pangs of birth,
new messiahs come and go to the cross,
a dusty man in the back rows
pushes his way to the front,
climbs the pulpit, and says,
'The crucified man was ours!
His blood is our heritage!'
Then he swallows all the ideals,
all that had caused calumny,
and spits them out as commentaries
and interpretations,
the last resort of helpless people,
maybe all people.
I look for the ideal man in vain.
People dream and ride the high winds,
then reach a stage when they weep bitterly
and break like branches.
They find loved ones,
who're the focus of their desires and lives,
then come to hate them
even while loving them still.

I hate her, she despises me.
But when we meet
in the loneliness, the darkness,
we become one whole, like a lump of kneaded clay,
hatred leaves, silence stays,
the silence that covered the earth
after it was created,
and we go on breaking
like branches.
We don't talk about the dreams we once dreamt,
we don't talk about the joys,
we simply go on breaking.
I'm fond of drinking,
she's addicted to smoking,
wrapped in a sheet of silence we cling to each other,
we go on breaking
like tender branches.

*Translated from Urdu by C.M. Naim and Vinay Dharwadker,
using earlier translations by Gopi Chand Narang and David
Paul Douglas, and Adil Jussawalla and the poet*

Devdas Chhotray (*b.* 1946)

Fear

What a kingdom you've brought me to!
A cold sun hangs at arm's reach,
a white eyeball. The wind writhes
helplessly like a fish hooked at the end of a line.
The street's festooned
with the naked corpses of boys
for the guest who'll arrive at high noon
in a red limousine.

Here I lie dressed, a white lily
wrapped in a silk scarf, the stars flickering;
your face appears, mournful in anguish;
what a country you've brought me to!
More intricate than the navel,
morning comes, hesitant and afraid,
like a guilty man.

If something shatters today,
if the street's flooded with a yellow viscous liquid,
if on this afternoon
a headless man arrives in a red limousine,
and if I tremble in fright,
impaled on a sharp star—
will you take me to your home again,
or hide me like an embryo in your womb?

Translated from Oriya by Jayanta Mahapatra

Kaifi Azmi (*b.* 1924)

Humiliation

When I left her door I thought
she'd try to stop me
            and we might be reconciled.
The wind billowed through our clothes;
I thought she'd ask me not to go,
and as she uncrossed her legs to get up
            I thought she'd come to call me back.
But she didn't try to stop me
and she didn't ask me to stay;
            she didn't call me
            and she didn't ask me to come back.
I walked away slowly
and the distance between us grew steadily,
            till our separation became finite.

Translated from Urdu by Mumtaz Jahan

Chandrashekhar Patil (*b.* 1939)

Freak

I shook myself awake, saw
the young sun gliding over the wall,
and went mad. I banged the door shut,
draped all the windows black,
and stuffed cotton in my ears
against the radio next door
shrieking out its morning songs.

I'd bought a flute once
to console my burnt and broken heart.
I broke it now in two. Made a bonfire
of all the movie songs on the shelf
and used the soot to draw moustaches
on the calendar pictures of the movie stars.
And laughed aloud to myself.

I walked in other people's gardens,
picked this, that, and the other flower,
pulled off the petals one by one,
piled them high and speared them through
with a long needle. Opened the lexicon,
picked out Soul, Truth, Goodness, Beauty,
and clapped them in dungeons of black ink.
Sentenced them to jail.

I entered the old castles of the heart.
Pulled out wishes and longings that lay dead,
or wriggled half-dead, or danced
wild on the stage, and threw them all out
for dogs, foxes, crows, and vultures
to peck at and live on. Saw them being eaten,
and was delighted at the sight.

I went out. I had my dark glasses on.
I walked right into the European-style hotel

that someone had said was very nice,
fell on a sofa, puffed away at dozens
of cigarettes, got drunk, muttered,
'This is the way the world ends,'
or something to that effect,
and went to sleep.

I don't know when, but I shook myself
awake again. A pair of liquid eyes
I'd loved once had got into my dream
somehow, and brought smiles to a dry mouth.
'Dear Fool, bow down before such freaks!'

Translated from Kannada by A.K. Ramanujan

Soubhagya Kumar Mishra (*b.* 1941)

Robinson Crusoe

The far, far sea (its waters blue and cool)
cast me mercifully on this island,
gave me supplies from the wrecked boat
and said: Build your home and live here.

But where is my home? And is anything here?
Uneven rock, bramble and shrub, gray sands,
no path to walk on, not a single companion
to talk to, no food; how can I live here?

Not a single tree, no shade, just the fiery sun;
a handful of dry leaves blow in the wind,
and join to the present those tender green memories:
here too there once were trees, and life, and flowers in bloom.

The old tobacco is stale;
not a single shoot grows from the barley I sow;
deprived of rain, the cracked salty earth
bares its huge teeth and mocks my efforts.

I accept silence here as law.
How helpless I am in this merciless prison!
Rocks lie about aimlessly;
the fatted sheep of my patience is sacrificed here.

No one pays heed to my cry of 'Brother, just a moment,'
as I walk the tarred road of this town;
I feel as homeless as Robinson Crusoe
thrown by fate on a deserted island.

And I watch cruel savages
tear and gnaw at each other's flesh and bone.
We gorge ourselves on meat and warm, raw blood;
why, then, this chant of glory, why this pious Thursday?

Translated from Oriya by Jayanta Mahapatra

Daya Pawar (*b.* 1935)

The Buddha

I never see you
in Jeta's garden,
sitting with your eyes closed,
meditating
in the lotus position,
or in the Ajanta and Ellora caves,
with your stone lips
sewn shut,
sleeping the last sleep of your life.
I only see you
walking, talking,
breathing gently, healingly,
on the sorrows of the poor
and the weak,
going from hut to hut
in the life-destroying darkness

with a torch in your hand,
giving their suffering—
which drains their blood
like a contagious disease—
a whole new meaning.

Translated from Marathi by Eleanor Zelliot
and Jayant Karve

Dilip Chitre (*b.* 1938)

My Father Travels

My father travels on the late evening train
Standing among silent commuters in the yellow light.
Suburbs slide past his unseeing eyes.
His shirt and pants are soggy, and his black raincoat
Is stained with mud, his bag stuffed with books
Is falling apart. His eyes dimmed by age
Fade homeward through the humid monsoon night.
Now I can see him getting off the train
Like a word dropped from a long sentence.
He hurries across the length of the grey platform,
Crosses the railway line and enters the lane.
His chappals are sticky with mud, but he hurries on.

Home again, I see him drinking weak tea,
Eating a stale chapati, reading a book.
He goes into the toilet to contemplate
Man's estrangement from a man-made world.
Coming out, he trembles at the sink,
The cold water running over his brown hands.
A few droplets cling to the greying hair on his wrists.
His sullen children have often refused to share
Jokes and secrets with him. He will now go to sleep
Listening to the static on the radio, dreaming
Of his ancestors and grandchildren, thinking
Of nomads entering a subcontinent through a narrow pass.

Vaidehi (*b.* 1945)

Girl in the Kitchen

Like other things
they say a kitchen too
means many things
but for this girl
this kitchen is her house
this that and every house
even the house of burial

Just as every creature
has a stomach
every house has a kitchen
I don't know whose plan it is
no windows no doors
not even a chimney for the smoke
not even a hole somewhere—
she longs for one

As she cooks—
the birds outside
the noise of playing children
buses cars autorickshaws running
into the distance
even to the seashore
but she ignores them
as she grinds the spices
renunciation comes easy
doesn't it
when you have nothing?

Yet sometimes if she hears
the airplane in the sky
the plane! the plane! she cries
from where she is
what trips can she take

while she's with salt and tamarind?
the twenty-first century?
will you take me with you?
the sound in the sky
melts away
v e r y   s l o w l y

This B.C. girl in the kitchen
blows *foo foo* into the fire
and sings
surely there's someone
up there in the plane
a gentleman in make-up and costume
as surely as all creatures are born
to steal and to cry

Maybe the flying chariot
will flap its wings
break through the roof
let down a ladder
lift me up as I peel potatoes
and make me the chief queen

O Rama Rama! carrying me
to Lanka or to Ayodhya?
old names and places
heard many times before
now what about worlds
no one has heard of?
fly to those worlds
I command you

And so on—
she weaves songs this girl
her ears open to the sounds in the sky
breaking the stalks of green peppers
her lifetime getting spent
drop by drop

Translated from Kannada by A.K. Ramanujan

Kamala Das (*b.* 1934)

Hot Noon in Malabar

This is a noon for beggars with whining
Voices, a noon for men who come from hills
With parrots in a cage and fortune cards,
All stained with time, for brown *kurava* girls
With old eyes, who read palms in light singsong
Voices, for bangle-sellers who spread
On the cool black floor those red and green and blue
Bangles, all covered with the dust of roads,
For all of them, whose feet, devouring rough
Miles, grow cracks on the heels, so that when they
Clambered up our porch, the noise was grating,
Strange. . . . This is a noon for strangers who part
The window-drapes and peer in, their hot eyes
Brimming with the sun, not seeing a thing in
Shadowy rooms, and turn away and look
So yearningly at the brick-ledged well. This
Is a noon for strangers with mistrust in
Their eyes, dark, silent ones who rarely speak
At all, so that when they speak, their voices
Run wild, like jungle-voices. Yes, this is
A noon for wild men, wild thoughts, wild love. To
Be here, far away, is torture. Wild feet
Stirring up the dust, this hot noon, at my
Home in Malabar, and I so far away. . . .

N. Balamani Amma (*b.* 1909)

To My Daughter

Daughter, lying on a snow-white bed
far away in a hospital,
are you weaving midnight into day
with the dark threads of pain?

Don't be depressed.
When we, too full of life,
rush about too much and need rest,
the Goddess of Creation offers us a sickbed.
Lie back, be refreshed; reinvigorate yourself.
There are so many steps still to be climbed.

Reading your poems in this dew-wet courtyard
I wonder whether the spirit in you,
which makes life blossom,
hurt you more than the body
that grew inside me like a flower.
These cocoons you've spun,
to put to sleep the worms
gnawing at your core,
burst open; and wings,
jostling, fluttering, rising,
swarm my mind.

Your mind may grow restless with unhappy thoughts,
your body may be weary of household tasks,
but I have no fears for you.
Your power to turn worms into butterflies
comforts me.

Translated from Malayalam by the poet

Meena Alexander (*b.* 1951)

Her Garden

The mountains crackle,
they are full of flint,
the cicada bristles,
it does not sing
in grandmother's garden,

as mulberry trees
gnarled like her hands
start their long slide
seawards.

I imagine her sitting
under the mulberry leaves,
hot fruit splashed
to her eyes,
a blindness cleaned
in that solitary hour
when trees clamber
out of their bark,
and swim
to a rock that is black
and bare
and like nothing
else in this homeland.

I like to think
she died in the daytime,
her face set heavenward
exacting little attention
from the sun:
once risen, it sets
in finicky chaos
in a sky so flat and blue
that light mirrors itself
as if on water, soundlessly:
so losing body,
she crept into her soul
and slept.

As young goats leap over breaches
in the garden wall,
as the cicada shunts sparks
from its wings,
I remember her.
She died so long
before my birth

that we are one, entirely,
as a sky
disowned by sun and star:
a bleakness beneath my dreams,
a rare fragrance,
as of dry mulberry
pierced by this monsoon wind.

V. Indira Bhavani (*b.* 1942)

Avatars

When he reads
smutty books
that foul the waters
        a contagion
            in the depths of society
and smacks his lips over them
in his own room
all alone
                he's the Fish

When he shrinks
inside his own shell
and hides himself
as others call upon him
to do good
strong deeds
                he's the Tortoise

When he falls flat
on his face
in an ocean of booze
and eagerly creates
a singular sort of world
                he's the Pig

At the office
when he makes the workers dance
and claws
    the files
    the men
    their work
to tatters
        he's Narasimha the man-lion

When his wishes
for underhand bribes
sprout and moulder
spore by spore
in a heart
full of cobwebs
        he's the Dwarf

When he weeds out
people he doesn't like
as he bears
his hoe-weapon
in his crooked heart
        he's Rama-with-the-axe

When he loudly takes the vow
of monogamy
in bed
and says
    Dear
    I'll never touch
    anyone else
    in this life
    not even in my heart
        he's Lord Rama

When he hides himself
behind dark glasses
enjoying women
fore and aft
on buses and off
      and takes special pleasure

in two separate houses
far apart
he's Lord Krishna

And so on and so forth
if you look more deeply
inside this man
you'll see
even a thousand
avatars there

But stand aside:
he's no less
than an avatar himself

Translated from Tamil by Martha Ann Selby

Popati Hiranandani (*b.* 1924)

Husband

This is my home.
I've touched you,
kissed you,
smelt you, enjoyed you.
That's why I keep you here.

This house
has polished floors
and expensive furniture.
A roof over your head,
four walls to protect you.
A kitchen,
a drawing room.
You cook for me.
I provide you
with two meals a day.

This home
has lively children.
They're my own blood.
They'll use my money,
make my name in the world,
and carry on my line.
When I'm dead and gone,
they'll propitiate my spirit
and feed me in the next world,
even if they don't
feed me in this one.

You're my children's mother,
that's why you're my wife.
If I give up my claim
to fatherhood,
you'll lose your claim
to this motherhood.
You belong to me—
I own everything that's yours.

With me
it's different.
I'm your husband.

Translated from Sindhi by the poet

Pranabendu Dasgupta (*b.* 1937)

Man: 1961

In a big wind, in a ruined house
trembling, he holds
with one hand the woman at his side,
while the other confuses him,
lacking a place to rest.
On a margosa tree the pigeons settle.

Facing a harrowing hill,
facing the darkness
of a heaving, wearisome sea,

he cannot find
a private view, a landscape of his own.

In a big wind, in a ruined house
he sways, he trembles.

Translated from Bengali by Buddhadeva Bose

K. Satchidanandan (*b.* 1946)

Genesis

My grandmother was insane.
As her madness ripened into death,
my uncle, a miser,
kept her in our store-room,
covered with straw.
My grandmother dried up, burst,
her seeds flew out of the windows.
The sun came, and the rain,
one seedling grew into a tree,
whose lusts bore me.

Can I help writing poems
about monkeys with gold teeth?

Translated from Malayalam by the poet

Saleem Peeradina (*b.* 1944)

Sisters

One, not quite ten
but ahead of the other, younger
whose five plus will never catch up
with the big one's lead
no matter how good she acts
or how hard she cheats.

Like any disadvantaged species
she has turned the handicap
in her favour: she's bolder,
sneakier, sweeter than honey,
obeyer of commands, underminer of rules,
producer of tears, yeller, complete

Turnaround. The older gets
the tough end of it. Most times
blames end up in her sullen face.
Fighting back, she argues, attacks
me for taking the wrong side.
I sweet talk her the way all parents

At all times have tried explaining
to the elder child. Living up
to her inheritance, she blazes back
at my moralizing. On bad days
I shout her down, immediately
regretting my words.

But even as she retreats
into a simmering silence, she stands her ground
knowing me to be unfair. Secretly,
I rejoice at the lesson never intended
but so well learnt: how to overcome
fathers, real and imaginary.

T.S. Venugopalan (*b.* 1929)

Family Pride

The rustic mango-stone
boasted of its pedigree.

I sowed it
and waited.
The huge tree and its fruits
turned into a shadow.
What wriggled out
was a worm.

Translated from Tamil by R. Parthasarathy

Benoy Majumdar (*b.* 1934)

Time Wins

I have lost this wager. Time wins.
It rained last night—or did I merely
Long for it in my sleep?
The rain now lies in pools, mirrors for the sky
To shave off its lather of clouds,
Fermenting mosquitoes, flies.

All that was delight and nourishment
In the mouth last night
Has turned into sordid history this pure morning,
Putrefaction in the crevices of the teeth
That no brushing can dislodge.
The blue stone on my ring simmers with unquenchable thirst.
I fear the day of my death will be one like this.

Translated from Bengali by Jyotirmoy Dutta

Gieve Patel (*b.* 1940)

Forensic Medicine

Text Book

A case in point, the expert says;
A woman thrust glowing faggots
Where properly
Her son's sparrow should nest.
Puerile in-law practice, he says,
But good as any other
To set the story rolling; begin
With a burn in the sparrow's nest
To extend over all therefrom emerging
Fan and flourish of the world:
Hold the foetus tumbling through,
And before it may express
Surprise at a clean new blast of air,
Lay subtle finger over mouth and nose.
Watch it blue.
If rather you would be coarse, go ahead,
Use rope and hatchet, knife, stone, bullet,
All you would on the more aged;
Bodies whose gel of blood and skin
Have exchanged years against sweet air
Will not relinquish with ease.
Against these devise infinite means,
The pictures in my book will instruct.
Change vantage point inch by inch
To discover them all: recall grace
Inherent in each new part, find
Weapon against it. Lop off limbs.
Smash teeth. Push splinters
Underneath nails and lever them
Off fingers; offer acid in a drink of wine,
The house of song is blasted. Soft skin
That clothes the gentlest dunes will retract

Before knife and bullet. Proceed.
Flick pages. The regal column of the neck
Upholding the globe of sight and sound
Is often undermined; or straight
Charge at speech and sight, chop off tongue,
Gouge eyeballs out, hammer nails into the ear.
When you have ravished all, missing
No entrail, do not forget
To return where you started: with a penknife
Strike at the rising sparrow's neck;
With ends of twine strangle the orbs
That feed him seed;
And outrage the sparrow's nest.

You are now full circle
With nothing
Not thought of, not done before.

Api

Another Me

Like a miracle song
in the womb of silence
he grows in me
perpetual embryo

appearing in me
he's the one who
shows me to myself
as someone new

like the wafting
of a southern breeze
in sandalwood forests
he moves always
in my poems

my dreams are all
dreamed in his sleep

my footprints
are pressed
under his passing feet

my inmost doors
are in his eyes

my depths
I fill with him

I let him glint
in my tears

he secretes honey
in my blossom

in my colourless skies
he's spread as the earth

it's he who has given me
wings

      as memory's curtain
      he hides the dark
      my past

      the future
      that's still in the womb
      he makes it grow
      feeding himself to it

Translated from Tamil by A.K. Ramanujan

Rajani Parulekar (*b.* 1945)

Birthmarks

The life of the nameless foetus
in the thick fluids
inside the womb:
so happy, so free.

Once we have cut the cord
and the child has taken in its first breath,
it has to grasp the messages
from the outside world,
even as it sends out its own.
When we interpret those sighs and gestures,
they become the sounds of a magical mantra:
one which brings the lifeless mind back to life,
like the breeze that comes straight off the sea,
carrying the green colour
of the foliage on the hill
spilt over into the lake.

Then, born once again,
we live through all the phases of life,
beginning with the stubborn, mischievous childhood;
the past's abrasions heal;
our soles are covered with layers of new skin,
to keep the stones ahead from hurting.
We meet the various shapes of our former lives
in a fresh light:
on the harsh night of the new moon
the obscure, mysterious, ugly forms among them
sit dozing and nodding like scarecrows
around bins of grain.
If we look at them with cruel eyes,
if we size them up with detachment,
they too come up with another standard
to measure the new life against.

And yet some birthmarks stay with us
in their original forms;
like blades of grass
they stir constantly in the bloodstream.
When, as a young girl,
I had spent three or four hours
making a festival pattern on the floor
with dry powdered pigments,
my mind would brim with a sense of fulfilment;
but realizing a moment later
that the pattern had to be wiped away the next day,
that it could not be framed like a picture,
I would be filled with anguish.

And even now,
when the darkness of death's world
slowly but surely
crowds into these four walls
and squats all night long in a corner
warming a vulture's eggs,
that sense of loss
tears itself from the past
and stands before me,
and the greenness that had spilt over
from the foliage on the hill into the lake
turns black and blue
like the blood congealed under the skin
on a badly bruised foot.

Translated from Marathi by Vinay Dharwadker

IV. The Master Carpenter

Sri Sri (1910–83)

from *Some People Laugh, Some People Cry*

(a prose poem)

A man walks on the bridge and gives away the change in his pocket to a beggar. He gives away his wristwatch to a nurse who happens to walk towards him. He throws his coat into the river and follows the coat into the water.

A man knows all the ins and outs of his trade. Rupee trees sprout in his palm. They lay golden eggs in banks. Tears drip from them like yolk.

A man sits silently near a milestone. He waits as if someone may arrive any minute. He eats peas as he counts buses. He forgets all time looking at a cloud.

A man wanders about carrying ladders—he has goose eggs in his bag. He leans his ladder against a wall. He climbs the ladder and throws an egg up into the sky. He is the same guy who bought Harishchandra for a heap of gold that high.

A man investigates holes. They differ in size.

A man offers anarchy for sale. He appears to be wading in space, searching for something with his long arms. He eats nothing but the giant lemon found in the lakes of blood in the hearts of the young. That too, only once a day.

A man spends time singing Raga Khamboji. It is not unnecessary to remind you that he has a lute with him. He has fingers only to legislate the ragas sung at appropriate times. At their touch stars catch fire. Lakes on the moon come to a boil. Winter begins to bud and my heart begins to offer marriage to the butterfly. A man puts camphor in his eyes and red lead on his cheeks. He is a poet. He interprets the messages he receives in secret code and works for the air force. He is the one big reason for the fall of prices in the market.

A man meditates with a string of *rudraksha* beads around his neck. What's the use of your knowing that there's no use in my pleading with people not to break coconuts in front of him?

A man loves only one woman. She dies. Follow the rest of the story on the silver screen.

A man gets hanged. Society buys peace with his death. The law sighs with relief. Every evening a blind dog visits the spot where his blood was spilled and barks piteously. This man was so proud he refused to say he was unjustly hanged.

A man becomes great by making speeches. Another becomes poor by drinking too much. One takes a copper from his maternal aunt and buys a kite. Another grabs it from him.

A man runs away. Another goes to Poona to perform fellatio. Another gets married. One man sleeps. Another dozes. Another talks and talks to while away time. One man's crying makes you laugh; another's laugh makes you cry. I can prove this with examples. . . .

Translated from Telugu by V. Narayana Rao
and A.K. Ramanujan

Arvind Krishna Mehrotra (*b.* 1947)

The Roys

We've rented a flat in Ghosh Buildings, Albert Road,
And the Roys live across the street. Mr Roy,
General Merchant, dresses in white
Drill trousers, long-sleeved cotton shirts,
And looks like a friendly barn-owl.
His sons are in school with me. Ganesh,

The eldest, has a gleaming forehead,
A shelled-egg complexion, a small
Equilateral mouth; he belongs to a mystical
Group of philatelists. Together with Shaporjee,
The tallow-white Parsi next door, and Roger Dutt,
The school's aromatic geography teacher, he goes up
In a hot-air balloon and, on the leeward
Side of a Stanley Gibbons catalogue, comes down
Near a turret in Helvetia or Magyar,
Stamp-sized snowflake-like countries
Whose names dissolve like jujubes on my tongue.
We play French cricket, seven-tiles, I-spy, and Injuns.
Our tomahawks are butter knives, our crow
Feathers are real, and riding out from behind
Plaza Talkies we ambush the cowboys of Civil Lines.
Ganesh doesn't join our games. The future,
He seems to say, is not a doodle on the back
Of an envelope but a scarp to be climbed
Alone. He attends a WUS meeting in Stockholm
And opens a restaurant in the heart of town.
I go there in early youth for Jamaican coffee,
In early middle age to use its toilet.
Without getting up from the cash desk he shakes my hand,
'How's the English Department?' he asks, 'How's
Rajamani? Is Mishra a professor now? Is it true? What are
things coming to?' While I listen to him
My piss travels down the left trouser leg
Into my sock, and then my restless son drags me
Towards a shoe store and buys his first pair of
Naughty Boys. Seen from the road,
Mr Roy's shop is a P & O liner anchored in midstream.
Inside, it's an abandoned coal pit. A film
Of darkness wraps the merchandise; a section of the far
Wall conceals the mouth of a cave, leading
To an underground spring; the air, dry and silvery
At the entrance, is moist and sea-green, furry
To the touch; the display cases, embedded
In the floor, are stuffed with a galleon's treasure;
Finned toffees peer at customers through glass jars.

Every afternoon Mr Roy goes home for his
Siesta and Ramesh, his second son, still wearing
A crumpled school uniform, takes over the town's
Flagship. At 3 p.m. the roads melt, becoming
Impassable, and canvas-backed chicks
Protect shop-fronts against heatstroke.
For the next two hours the sun, stationed above
A traffic island, lays siege to the town, and the only
Movement is of leaves falling
So slowly that midway through their descent their colours
Change. The two waxen shop-assistants
Melt in their sticks, Ramesh sits beside
The cash box with an open sesame
Look in his eye, and I have the well
All to myself. Looking up its bejewelled
Shaft, I make out, in the small
Light coming in through the well-mouth,
Bottles of ketchup, flying cigarillos,
Death-feigning penknives, tooth powders, inexpensive
Dragon china dinner sets, sapphire-blue packets
Of detergent, wooden trays holding skeins
Of thread, jade-coloured boxes of hosiery, rolled-gold
Trinkets, mouth-watering dark tan shoe polish, creams
And hula hoops. Driven by two ceiling fans,
The freighter moves. Land drops from sight.
Though binoculars are trained on the earth's dip,
The eye is monopolized by afterimages of land:
I hold a negative against the light,
And now I'm received into the negative I'm holding.
At 5 p.m. the spell is broken. The sun
Calls it a day and goes down and Mr Roy comes
To clear away the jungle that has grown around his shop and I
Run out with a stolen packet of razor blades.
Where stealing's easy, hiding stolen goods is tough.
A pink stamp issued on Elizabeth's coronation
Cannot be traced to a cigarette tin buried among
Clothes, but what do I do with an album that has
The owner's name rubber stamped
All over it? I give lessons to five-year-old Suresh

In the pleasures of stealing.
For each first-day cover he brings, I press
My View-Master against his mongoloid eye
and let him look through it once. Then one day, while we're
Having lunch, I see a policeman framed in the door.
The food in my mouth hardens into a lump
Of plaster of Paris. Afterwards, I lose my voice
And so does everyone around me. Believe me when I say
There's nothing more sad than a tropical evening,
When auctioneers buy dead advocates' libraries
And there's all the time in the world and nowhere to go.
Anil, their cousin, takes out his autograph-book.
'Just in case,' he says, 'you become famous.'
He has said this to every boy in school.
'Do you think,' he asks me, 'I can get Peeks's
Grandfather's autograph?' Peeks's grandfather is a retired
Chief Justice and gets his pension in sterling.
Anil squints at a marble
In the hollow of his palm
But can't make out if it's an oblong. His sister, hairy
As a sloth bear, sits in the verandah, absorbed
In our game. Her mind, too, is half her age.
Through broken tiles in the roof
Sunbeams let themselves down and she screams
Before they strike her. She vanishes
Inside a blackbeetle and crawls on my skin;
I smell the bouquet of my spittled thumb
And it works like hartshorn. Charlie Hyde, nicknamed
Bony Arse, is the only other person
To so affect me. We go our different ways and sometimes
We cross Albert Road together or meet outside
A chemist's. Anil has a tabletop head and bulging
Irisless eyes. He nods; I nod. It's like watching
From a distance two men one doesn't know
Recognize each other. Anil sets himself up
As a dealer in office equipment
And then as a distributor for Number Ten cigarettes.
He fails at both jobs and is given shock therapy.

Shrikant Verma (1931–86)

The Pleasure Dome

—And as I walk along, thinking of this,
a bullet whizzes past·
                                    very close to me.
Is this a holdup,
or is it a revolution?
Whatever it is, it makes no difference now,
all that's left for me to do
is to move along.
I've watched the country on the map,
every year the map's different,
a portion to China,
another to Pakistan—
                              just then
the second bullet,
the same resounding BANG!

This is really the limit, I'll have to speak out now,
there seems to be no limit to anything,
you might as well come right in,
                                        strip me to the skin,
lash me on the butt and write across my face
HE'S AN ASS.
                    Even this
makes no difference—
everyone sits leashed exactly where he is,
keeping every strand of shameless indifference in place
with a cheap plastic comb.

Go on, go right ahead,
in the whorehouses, on the sleeping mats, in hell,
on the ruined towers with their dingy stairs,
strangle them—
                        those giggly affairs, those writhing lusts,
that anger mounting and rearing at every turn,
what difference do they make?

                              I empty myself out each time
only to be filled with still more pus.

Whether it's running sores or eczema, acne or ringworm,
it works wonders on all of them,
this SURDAS CREAM from Mathura,
try it now,
                    today.
What did you say? Salamander oil
to give me staying power?
No, no, sweet ladies eager to be laid, please turn back,
I'm past such things,
                              I've let them pass just like that,
let everything return to its proper place,
        sins to the world,
            con-men to their mothers' wombs,
            bureaucrats to their gymkhanas,
            politicians
                    to their smelly stables.

The monsoon isn't going to arrive,
there's going to be a shortage of grain,
everyone's going to die of indigestible NEWS,
only the capital's going to survive.
The stomach's already begun to convulse,
go get yourself inoculated with ghee,
its price has gone up alarmingly,
it's twice what it used to be,
one feels the emptiness,
                    the sap's gone.

What did you say? No, no,
this cream's guaranteed to work
on eczema, on acne, on ringworm. . . .

—No matter who runs the show, I go by no one else's terms,
listen to no one's pleas
                    that he killed my enemy.
No one represents me,
before the census count
I must pass away from every lane in every town,

    every ballot-box will contain
    one vote less,
no one makes the terms for me.

I have to make my way through the milling crowd,
I have to pass the mass of flies,
drawing close to them, one by one,
I have to move away from all my friends,
YOU THERE, WALK PROPERLY,   •
this Absurdity barks at me—
shoving me around,
surrounding me with eyes that glare,
where are you taking me against my will?
Let go! let go! let go of me,
or else!
      Nothing else after this
except a bus-stop
that faces no one, nothing.
Turn me too into a stop,
I've been left to wander
till the end of time,
          raving.

O Honorary Surgeon,
Consultant,
CONSULTATION HOURS 5 TO 7,
redeem me, let me go—
my taste has been changing steadily,
living here this long
even I have begun to belong,
the evening's coming on,
change, change those hours you keep,
these times are not those times.

Sorrows, exchanges,
remaindered inventories,
strikes and accidents, traffic in women,
the proletariat of the Communists,
the common people of the Jana Sangh,
mourning for things not done,

mourning for what was done,
                           all these have converged
on the senseless death of the eunuch Khudabakhsh,
embodiment of God's mercies.
                    Let the criminal courts convene!
You've got away with things conveniently so far,
to tell you the truth, I couldn't see you this time
for what you are. God only knows
from what bygone days they're coming down,
what rooftops, what beds, what stairs,
in tandem,
              the women beaten blue,
sickly pale, fucked dry,
trying to take in the final scene.

The palmist juggles the future on a fingertip,
the merchant stows it in his safe.
                           Three years ago
they caught one Stupid Singh for a theft—
but the true story breaks out only now.

Once out, it feels free, but otherwise
it's frightening,
                    the hundredth one who passes by
seems the exemplar of spring.
Am I the keeper of the straggling ninety-nine
caught in the bind of greed
that grows and grows?
At any rate,
              it's too late now,
a conference of crows has settled on the map
spread like a patterned cloth for chequers.
The earth's being portioned out—

on this occasion, give me leave to crow,
forgive me,
              let me go,
what's there left to be freed, anyhow—
                    one more cold immersion,
                    another enchantment broken,

though everything went against me,
I made poems possible,
made something of myself,

                          THANKS!

The misbegotten one,
and not the one of noble rank,
breaks the status quo.
Everything's broken,

                    only Shiva's bow,
weighed in gold for the suitors' contest,
doesn't break.

            What difference will weeping make—
saying this, the widow yawns and goes to bed,
who's humped all day
by the toll-keeper, trader in buffaloes.

Does Time see all this, or doesn't it?
I have my doubts.

                This man has his gonorrhoea,
that one, his diabetes.
The fear of extinction appears again
and again the lineage peters out. . . .

Shall I pass from here like this,
completely disengaged?

                Forgive me, Lord, I'll make
my decision in the morning,
when the decision will have been made.

Translated from Hindi by Vinay Dharwadker
and Aparna Dharwadker

G. Shankara Kurup (1901–72)

The Master Carpenter

I feel a little better today.
But how long shall I lie
coiled here?
The marrow of my bones is gouged out and eaten.
I'm a mere ghost. I just breathe.

This is April.
The jackfruit tree that shines
like slashed gold at the touch of a chisel,
and the honey-mango tree that always tempts the hand
to carve a toy boat from its trunk,
will be shaking now
with blossom, with fruit.
If only I could creep up to the window
and take a look at them!
There's not a plantain stump in my garden,
and my heart beats when I see a tree,
any tree, anywhere.

That single champak tree near the Uliyannur temple.
O it's huge, it's so straight.
Nine men can't hug it with joined hands.
No bend, no crack, not a hole in it, not a hole.
I can measure it with my eyes:
it's more than eighty *kols.*
If you cut it down, you can change the bamboo thatch
of every mother's son in the village.
Or else we could make rafters for houses
that would be the envy of the chieftains.
But this stump's now rotten.
What's the use of wishing for things?
I can't even sink the edge of my chisel
into any wood any more.

Nani, she sits on the doorstep,
her stomach caved in, bent double,
fumbling for bits and pieces of dry betel leaf,
a chunk of betel nut, a stalk of tobacco.
Fire a cannon in her ear, she won't hear it.
She's an old crone now.
I remember the day she stood by my side,
straight as a champak tree in bloom,
a body fresh from under the chisel,
her smile a sparkle of new silver.

> The old eyes came out of the gray bush of the eyebrows,
> went out through the back door all eaten up by white ants
> and wandered there for a while.
> 'If only I could get up, I could crawl.
> O the hand that could have held up an old man. . . .'
> The old carpenter shook with sobs.
> As if to wipe it all away, memory and all,
> his hand passed slowly over the furrows on his forehead.

If only I could somehow totter up to the workshop,
I could at least sit there,
and taste the gladness
that only scale and chisel can bring.

That temple, like a huge inverted bowl
carved in black wood, shining under the sky—
it rose under these working hands.
With my chisel I put in his hands,
my child made that sacred eagle now there
on the flagmast of burnished brass,
and those wings that look as if they're moving.

> They say I'm green with envy.
> What father won't beam with pride
> on hearing the praises of his son?
> But then, you can stop the clappers of a thousand bells,
> but you can't stop one wagging tongue.
> We two made teakwood images
> of the guardsmen of the eight directions,
> and placed them on the twin towers:

one made with this hand, the other with his.
They said his image had more life than mine.
My son wins, but what does it matter
for a father to lose to his son?
Isn't his glory my glory too?

But look, they said, my face darkened
to hear the boy praised.
I may be a carpenter, but am I not also a father?
They said, the old man knows the carpentry and the craft,
but it's the son who has the sculptor's art.
Why should these village idiots gabble like this?
We sat near each other at work in the shop,
but there was silence between us.
Let them slight me and say what they will.

Can I, can I, his real father,
really wish for this dreadful end?
He may be clever, may even be a genius,
but he got it all from his father.
That old Nayar said, when I went to his house,
'When the moon arrives, the sun must fade.'
Why did he have to say such things?

Once, for fun, I made a moving doll
and fixed it below the bridge.
At the first footfall the doll would dance like a water goddess;
when a man came to the middle of the bridge,
she would come up on the water inch by inch
and open her mouth and spit
at the unsuspecting man,
taking him completely by surprise.
There were milling crowds at the river to see this wonder.

Young sandalwood trees emit their fragrance
if they are chafed,
but, let me tell you,
my child proved his mettle against mine
without scorn or ill-will.
In four days, another doll rose in his name

on the lips of the people everywhere.
When my doll came up to spit,
his doll would slowly turn and lift her hand;
and when mine opened her mouth to spit,
his would slap her smartly in the face.
I felt that slap.
Even in the sky there isn't room enough for two moons.
He left the house. Nani was in tears.
My heart burned inside me like a heap of paddy husk,
but I held my tongue.

Then came the elephant pandal for the temple.
Why on earth did I have to call
on this great son of mine for it?
My master said to me,
'Consult your son and make the pandal beautiful.'
I felt like turning back at once.
But I didn't.
Consult! No one so far had said that to me.

It might look like envy.
But isn't a son's glory the father's?
Though the carpenter may work with wood,
he himself isn't wood.
The pandal came up well.

As you know, a pandal needs artistic work on the facade.
He said, 'I'll look after that, if you wish,
and my father can work on putting up the gables.'
Does he, my son, have to tell me,
his father, to put up the gables?
Do I need his nod for this?

His hands were working
on Goddess Lakshmi's lotus,
carving a sandal.
And I was shaping a wooden rivet
with the broad chisel,
its blade glittering in the sun
like the edge of a sword.
And then, unawares,

unawares it slipped out of my hand,
that chisel!

I began to pray at once
and begged of God that it shouldn't fall on my son.

In the flick of an eyelash
I saw my son reeling to the ground,
head almost severed from body.
People gathered around.
Eyes, like long sharp needles, looked at me.
How could I find my feet on the ladder?
I somehow plunged to the ground.
It seems my son then said, 'Forgive me.'
I didn't hear the words.
Curly hair gummed to the neck with blood,
in blood he lay.
Those staring eyes
that had swallowed all pain, that sight
is always with me, it doesn't leave me.

And no one has seen Nani smile since then.
Scalding tears flowed from her eyes
till they could flow no more.
Who will believe that it was a slip of the hand?
Whatever one might say, who will ever believe it?

O Nani, you don't believe it, do you,
will a father ever do this?
My son would now have been the staff of my life,
if only it hadn't happened.
'Happened? Made to happen!'
a little voice says inside me,
correcting me again and again.
Can a father do it?
Something hammers away at my heart with a mallet,
something tries to pull out that nail
hammered in so deep.

> Nani broke the old man's chain of memories
> as she pounded away at her little hand-mill

of betel leaf and betel nut,
'It's some time since those cobwebs
were swept from the ceiling.
Did something fall into your eyes?
Why're they watering?'

Translated from Malayalam by K.M. George
and A.K. Ramanujan

V. What Is Worth Knowing?

Labhshankar Thacker (b. 1935)

Poem

> The word is fast asleep
> under the blanket of the adjective.
> Shall I wake it up?

Translated from Gujarati by Sitanshu Yashashchandra

Sujata Bhatt (b. 1956)

What Is Worth Knowing?

That Van Gogh's ear, set free
wanted to meet the powerful nose
of Nevsky Avenue.
That Spain has decided to help
NATO. That Spring is supposed to begin
on the 21st of March.
That if you put too much salt in the *keema*
just add a few bananas.
That although the Dutch were the first
to help the people of Nicaragua they don't say much
about their history with Indonesia.
That Van Gogh collected Japanese prints.
That the Japanese considered
the Dutch to be red-haired barbarians.
That Van Gogh's ear remains full of questions
it wants to ask the nose of Nevsky Avenue.
That the vaccinations for cholera, typhoid and yellow fever
are no good—they must be improved.
That red, green and yellow are the most
auspicious colours.
That turmeric and chilli powder are good
disinfectants. Yellow and red.

That often Spring doesn't come
until May. But in some places
it's there in January.
That Van Gogh's ear left him because
it wanted to become a snail.
That east and west
meet only in the north and south—but never
in the east or west.
That in March 1986 Darwinism is being
reintroduced in American schools.
That there's a difference
between pigeons and doves, although
a ring-dove is a wood-pigeon.
That the most pleasant thing is to have a fever
of at least 101—because then the dreams aren't
merely dreams but facts.
That during a fever the soul comes out
for fresh air, that during a fever the soul bothers to
speak to you.
That tigers are courageous and generous-hearted
and never attack unless provoked—
but leopards,
leopards are malicious and bad-tempered.
That buffaloes too,
water-buffaloes that is, have a short temper.
That a red sky at night is a good sign for sailors,
for sailors . . . what is worth knowing?
What is worth knowing?

Kaa Naa Subramanyam (*b.* 1912)

Situation

Introduced
to the Upanishads
by T.S. Eliot;

and to Tagore
by the early
Pound;

and to the Indian Tradition
by Max Mueller
(late of the Bhavan);

and to
Indian dance
by Bowers;

and to
Indian art
by what's-his-name;

and to the Tamil classics
by Danielou
(or was it Pope?):

neither flesh
nor fish blood
nor stone totem-pole;

vociferous
in thoughts
not his own;

eloquent in words
not his own
('The age demanded . . . .').

Translated from Tamil by the poet

Amrita Pritam (*b.* 1919)

The Creative Process

The poem looks at the paper
And turns her face away,
As if the paper were a strange man, not her own.

But when a virgin keeps the fast of *karva chauth*,
And on that dreamlike night
Feels a male touch in a dream
Suddenly her body shivers.

But sometimes, tasting that fire
Startled, she awakes.
She touches her lush body
And undoes her blouse,
Splashes a handful of moonlight over her body.
Her hand sobs as she dries her body.

The darkness of her body spreads out like a mat.
Lying face-down on the mat, she picks at straws,
Every limb of her body catches fire.
She feels as if her body's darkness longs
To be crushed in powerful arms.

Suddenly, paper appears before her
And touches her trembling hands.
One part of her body burns,
Another melts,
She smells a strange odour
And her hand reads the throbbing lines of her body.
Her hands grow drowsy,
Her body becomes a total stranger.
She breaks into a cold sweat.
A long line breaks—
Her breath is drenched in the smell of life and death.
All these thin black lines,
Like pieces of a drawn-out scream.

Silent, puzzled,
Drained,
She stands and looks.
As if some injustice had been committed,
Some small part of her had died.
As if a virgin had conceived
And then miscarried.

Translated from Punjabi by the poet and Arlene Zide

Savithri Rajeevan (*b.* 1955)

A Pair of Glasses

It's with glasses
in front of my eyes and on my nose
that I see the world.

I need glasses
to see my neighbour and the washerman
and the postman,
to see that Radha and Krishna walking along the road,
or to see Radha as Radha
and Krishna as Krishna.

Glasses are the door
through which I talk to a stranger,
a guest, a friend.
Through their glass I speak
to children, flowers,
and God.

Glasses for my day-dreams,
and for my cradle-songs.

For my unspoken word
and my unsung song.
Glasses.
Glasses for me.

In my childhood
I had no glasses.
All great men wear glasses.
All wearers of glasses are great.
My childhood—without glasses.
The textbook Gandhiji,
the cane-wielding math teacher,
and Appunni, the postman.
Or, for that matter,
behind every pair of glasses that's taken off
a great man.
In my childhood
I had no glasses.

But today,
like the gods and prophets
who have haloes,
the scholar who has a bald head,
or the rich man who has a potbelly,
I too have
a pair of glasses.

Translated from Malayalam by K. Ayyappa Paniker
and Arlene Zide

Kabita Sinha (*b.* 1931)

The Diamond of Character

From the eyes endlessly falls
All that isn't the eye, isn't vision,
    All that's insubstantial;
From the lips falls all that isn't worth expressing:
Words, sounds, kisses;
From the heart falls the mind's true worth,
    All that isn't one's own.

Just as with a flower in its proper season
All that isn't the flower's falls away,
So the brightly coloured petals fall
    In the same patterns.
Come back to my face, you lines of sorrow,
Come back from beyond the cycle of birth and rebirth,
Breaking through sorrow and betrayal,
The terrible humiliations;
Come back, pushing through the black hair,
    O purity's pallor:
Now, casting off beauty's gleam, youth's blaze,

I want to take up the diamond of character.

Translated from Bengali by Swapna Mitra
and Carolyne Wright

Gnanakoothan (*b.* 1938)

Tamil

Tamil, it's true, is the breath of my life.
But I won't breathe it down my neighbour's neck.

Translated from Tamil by A.K. Ramanujan

Raghuvir Sahay (1929–90)

Our Hindi

Our Hindi is a widower's new wife
she talks too much eats too much sleeps too much

Go on making ornaments for her
keep giving her a swollen head

Let her get fat let her smell of sweat
let her keep smuggling the stuff out to her mother's

Let her burn with envy for her neighbours
let her quarrel over garbage disposal

Of course the question of turning her out of the house
    doesn't arise
everything a woman needs is in the house
a Mahabharata a Ramayana one by Tulsidas and one
    by Radheshyam
the story of the film 'Nagin' including the lyrics for all
    its songs
and a Kokshastra printed in Khari Baoli

There's a stupid maid for the mess of household things
a middle-aged husband to pick on and strip naked
an untended garden several rooms like cells inside each other
soiled pillows on the bed crumpled clothes on the chairs
glasses tumbling on the floor
dirty linen on the pegs to be taken and washed at the well

Everything a woman needs is in the house
dankness and five kilograms of gold in the inner room
a child with an enlarged liver
whom she teaches to squat over the monthly magazines
a plot of land on which our Hindi Bhavan will be built

Let the faultfinders say what they will
our Hindi is a married woman she's faithful she's happy
she wants to die before her husband dies
everything's okay but first her husband must survive her
for how else can she have her wish

Translated from Hindi by Vinay Dharwadker

Siddhalinga Pattanshetti (b. 1939)

Woman

Woman
is a problem negative:
print it,
enlarge it, do what you will,
as you rub the chemicals
of desire,
the picture, the same old picture,
gets clearer and clearer.

Translated from Kannada by A.K. Ramanujan

Bahinabai Chaudhari (1880–1951)

The Naming of Things

(an oral folk poem)

If it doesn't open up,
Don't call it a pod of cotton.

If it doesn't call out Hari's name,
Don't call it a mouth.

If it doesn't stir in the breeze,
Why call it a leaf?

If it doesn't hear Hari's name,
Don't call it an ear.

If it doesn't have wells or water-channels,
Don't call it an orchard.

If it hasn't seen God's image,
Don't call it an eye.

If it makes you sleep on an empty stomach,
Don't call it night.

If it refuses to give,
Don't call it a hand.

If it doesn't run with water,
Why call it a stream?

If they walk away from cries of help,
Don't call them feet.

If it comes up empty from the well,
Don't call it a bucket.

If it feeds only itself,
Just call it a belly.

If she doesn't recognize her calf,
Don't call her a cow.

If her breasts don't flow with milk,
Don't call her a mother.

No, the rope lying on the path—
don't ever call it a snake.

If a man sells his daughter,
Don't call him a father.

If the milk has curdled,
Don't call it cream.

If her love can disappear,
Don't call her a mother.

If he's ungrateful to his parents,
Don't call him a son.

If it doesn't contain any feeling,
Why call it devotion?

If it doesn't contain a real goal,
Don't call it strength.

Adapted by Vinay Dharwadker from
'What It Should Not Be Called',
translated from Marathi by
Philip Engblom and Jayant Karve

Nabaneeta Dev Sen (*b.* 1938)

The Yellow River

the great wall of china
rises inside
blocking stars
woods ricefields

the great wall of china rises within
blocking everything

yet
the yellow river
sweeps away village
after village

Translated from Bengali by the poet

Sadanand Rege (1923–82)

Old Leaves from the Chinese Earth

(I bought a Chinese book at a second-hand book shop. I got a
man who spoke Japanese to explain it to me. All that I could
make out of it is what follows.)

I am Chiang Liang.
Once I was crossing the bridge,
And an old man was sitting there.
As soon as he saw me,
He took off one of his shoes
And threw it deliberately into the river,
And said to me:
My good fellow,
My shoe has fallen into the river,
Please fish it out for me.
I was furious.
But I curbed my temper
And jumped into the water.
As soon as I had come up with the shoe,
He threw the other into the river.
'Oh, there goes the other one too.'
I dived into the water again
And came back with the second shoe,
When he threw the first one back into the river.
I was furious. He said:
Meet me here again after thirteen years.

After thirteen years
There was no one on the bridge.
Only the sun blazed down on it,
The size of a tiger's jaw.
I waited a long time for the old man.
Then I came down and looked into the water:
There was my own face behind the sun,
There was nobody on the bridge except the sun.

But someone spoke out of my bones:
One shoe is life, the other is death.
I recognized the voice.

Translated from Marathi by Dilip Chitre

K. Ayyappa Paniker (*b.* 1930)

The Itch

> my first itch
> came to squat on my right knee.
> my last itch
> leaned on my left knee.
> shan't we scratch, o my people,
> shan't we scratch?
>
> some say
> the world was born
> of a divine itch.
> others say
> the lord himself
> was born of an itch.
> the disputationists!
> all i know is this—
> the pleasure
> of scratching an itch.
> all else
> may be illusion,
> but this is truth eternal.

Translated from Malayalam by the poet

Khalil-ur-Rahman Azmi (1927–78)

I and 'I'

The day's exhaustion brings me to the valley of sleep;
A bed of dust is better than any bed of roses.
Bring on the night, put out all the lights:
The body will sleep, and so will the mind.

But night has come, and the lights are still on.
A fire is still smouldering in my side.
Every hair on my body tells me, 'Go,
Go find the one thing you've lost.'

I run out of the house, barefoot,
I beat my head against the ground and cry,
'O you gods, give me back my submission—
Or else my demon won't let me sleep.'

Translated from Urdu by C.M. Naim
and Norman H. Zide

Nara (b. 1932)

White Paper

A great man once said to me:
write whatever you want to,
but on the condition—
it should be an improvement
on the blank white page.

Blank white paper
is more important
than what I write now.
My poetry
is in the white spaces
between the words.

Like news about the men
who disappeared before dawn,
like seeds buried in the soil,
like the truth that hides
between the heavy headlines,
like a fragrant green flower,
the more I write
the more poetry there is

in the white spaces between the words.

Translated from Telugu by V. Narayana Rao

Subramania Bharati (1882–1921)

Wind, 9

Wind, come softly.
Don't break the shutters of the windows.
Don't scatter the papers.
Don't throw down the books on the shelf.
There, look what you did—you threw them all down.
You tore the pages of the books.
You brought rain again.
You're very clever at poking fun at weaklings.
Frail crumbling houses, crumbling doors, crumbling rafters,
crumbling wood, crumbling bodies, crumbling lives,
crumbling hearts—
the wind god winnows and crushes them all.
He won't do what you tell him.
So, come, let's build strong homes,
let's joint the doors firmly.
Practise to firm the body.
Make the heart steadfast.
Do this, and the wind will be friends with us.

The wind blows out weak fires.
He makes strong fires roar and flourish.
His friendship is good.
We praise him every day.

Translated from Tamil by A.K. Ramanujan

Shakti Chattopadhyay (*b.* 1933)

Forgive Me

The jar containing vermilion
Crashes on the hard edge
Of the table.
It crashes every day.
It rains every day—continuously.
The noise spreads
And is absorbed by an ocean
Where colour is louder than sound,
Where harmony is greater than colour.
Only the original note sounds there,
And leaves an imprint on her heart of sand.
She floods my face with saliva.
She rests her hand on my shoulder and whispers—
Forgive me: you cannot play me any more.

Translated from Bengali by Prithvindra Chakravarty
and Ulli Beier

Chennavira Kanavi (b. 1928)

On Bismillah Khan's Shehnai

With one breath he makes the place green,
scatters flowers in an eddy of winds,
and floats perfumes; he listens to the voice
of wishes; from the heart's centre,
he makes rainbows that span earth and sky.
Lightning breaks through the clouds,
the waters of music rush seaward,
and the ears throb with pulses
from nebulae light years away.
As the earth hangs from a thread of sound,
the sun and the moon swing, skylights
open in the caves of the netherworld.
As the *shehnai* cuts the cord at the navel,
the sky breaks and life opens its mouth.

Translated from Kannada by A.K. Ramanujan

Shahryar (b. 1936)

Still Life

Flowers leaves stems
lips hands eyes

Wave of blood heart sound
moonlight sun

All these are frozen

There's not a single arrow
in time's bow

Translated from Urdu by Gopi Chand Narang
and David Paul Douglas

Arun Kolatkar (*b.* 1932)

The Alphabet

anvil arrow bow box and brahmin
cart chariot cloud and compost heap
are all sitting in their separate squares

corn cup deer duck and frock
ganesh garlic hexagon and house
all have places of their own

inkpot jackfruit kite lemon and lotus
mango medicine mother old man and ostrich
are all holding their proper positions

pajamas pineapple rabbit and ram
sacrifice seal spoon and sugarcane
won't interfere with each other

sword tap tombstone and umbrella
warrior watermelon weight and yacht
have all found the eternal resting place

the mother won't put her baby on the compost heap
the brahmin won't season the duck with garlic
the yacht won't hit the watermelon and sink

unless the ostrich eats the baby's frock
the warrior won't shoot an arrow into ganesh's belly
and if the ram doesn't knock down the old man

why would he need to smash the cup on the tombstone

Translated from Marathi by Vinay Dharwadker

VI. The Doe in Heat

B.R. Lakshman Rao (*b.* 1946)

Green Snake

Early morning, the day before yesterday,
under a slab of stone,
in a crack,
eyes glittering,
forked tongue licking and flashing,
a frog swelling his belly,
he lay there quietly:
a baby snake, two hands long,
a green snake.

'Poor thing. It's a green snake. Still a baby.
What harm can it do?' I said.
My father replied,
'A snake's a snake.'
And mother,
'That's where everyone walks.
We don't need trouble. Kill it.'
'I can't,' I said.

Father struck him with a piece of firewood,
chased him outside,
and killed him flat.

Translated from Kannada by A.K. Ramanujan

Paresh Chandra Raut (*b.* 1936)

Snake

Once in a dream I saw a snake
in a gun barrel's steely braid.
The fears of childhood kept pursuing me in tales of snakes:
in ruined houses, brick-stacks and drains, on river banks

I imagine a snake, its fangs packed with poison,
slide stealthily toward me whenever I am alone.
In the dark, derelict graves of the old English cemetery,
under the hangman's banyan tree on the Mahanadi bank,
it bears down on my throat
as it swings joyfully from the branch of a guava tree.

And the snake pulls the noose around my neck,
fires a gun, attacks my legs—
for had I been awake, I could have saved myself,
but in a nightmare I can never make my escape,
no charm or mantra will ever come to my mind;
the ropes of the snake trip up my feet.

And in another dream
I saw I was the first being in the garden of Eden:
Adam's full likeness, with Eve my beloved—
but the next instant found Eve lying dead,
her body purple with poison.
So I called for the doctor, only to discover
the physician was God himself, the great Healer,
his signature evident everywhere in the garden.
I realized then that it was the work of the tempter,
        the snake;
from that day on the snake was my foe,
from that day on I was his death.

And I found I had become limbless again, stripped of attire;
I saw the snake in my limb, symbol of my manhood,
saw the slow slink of sin, and was stunned;
I saw the sharp fangs in my mouth,
saw the various mouths of my own testimony,
my urge slithering along the ground;
saw my innumerable desires
turned into innumerable little snakes,
and saw them rebel, striking one another and my body,
as I burned in the fires of my own venom—
the few untrained eagles of my ways
could not keep the situation in check;
for I saw myself as a snake in my dreams,

and saw the mark of the snake on my own flesh
in the subconscious of Eden's ruins.

Translated from Oriya by Jayanta Mahapatra

Nirmalprabha Bardoloi (*b.* 1933)

Dawn

Does the day break
with the sound of guns?
No,
it breaks with the cry
of that bird
which nibbles through
the night's darkness
very slowly.

Translated from Assamese by D.N. Bezbarua

Jibanananda Das (1899–1954)

In Camp

Here, on the forest's edge, I have pitched camp.
All night long, in the pleasant southern breezes,
in the light of the moon in the sky,
I hear the call of the doe in heat—
whom is she calling?

Somewhere tonight the deer are being hunted.
The hunters came to the forest today—
I too catch their scent

as I lie here on my campbed,
wide awake
on this spring night.

The wonder of the forest is everywhere,
an April breeze,
like the taste of the moon's rays.
All night long the doe calls in heat.
Deep in the forest somewhere, in places the moonlight does
    not reach,
all the stags hear her call;
they sense her presence,
they move towards her.
Tonight, on this night of wonder,
their time for love has come.
The sister of their hearts calls them through the moonlight
from their forest cover
to quench their thirst, by smell, by taste.
Tonight, as if the forest were free of tigers,
no sharp fear, not even a shadow of doubt,
fills the heart of those deer—
only thirst,
excitement.
Perhaps wonder awakens even in the cheetah's breast
at the beauty of the doe's face.
Tonight, on this night of spring,
lust, longing, love, desire, dreams burst all around.
This is my 'nocturne'.

The deer come, one by one, leaving the dense forest trails,
leaving behind the sounds of water in search of a different
    assurance,
forgetting tooth and claw, they come there in the moonlight
to their sister under the *sundari* tree.
Those deer come like a man who draws near his salty woman
    lured by her scent.
—I sense them,
I hear the sound of numerous hooves,
the doe in heat is calling through the moonlight.
I cannot sleep.

As I lie here,
I hear gunshots.
Once more I hear the sound of guns.
Once more the doe in heat calls in the moonlight
as I lie here fallen alone,
a weariness swells my heart
as I listen to the sound of guns
as I hear the doe call.

She will come back tomorrow.
We will see her by daylight in the morning
with all her lovers lying dead around her.
She has learnt all this from men.

I will smell venison on my dinner plate.
            —Hasn't the eating of flesh come to an end?
            —But why should it end?
Why should I be pained at the thought of those deer—
am I not like them?
On a spring night,
on one of life's wondrous nights,
did someone not come into the moonlight and call me too—
in the pleasant southern breezes,
like that doe in heat?
Has not my heart, a stag,
wanted to hold you with all caution thrown aside,
forgetting all the violence of this world,
forgetting the fear of the cheetah's gaze?
When the love in my heart
lay smeared with blood and dust, like those dead deer,
did you not live on like that doe
through life's wondrous night
one night in spring?

Even you have learnt it from someone.
We too lie here with our flesh like the flesh of dead beasts.
Like those dead deer
everyone comes, then falls
in the face of separation and death.
By living, loving, longing for love,

we are hurt, we are embittered, we die,
do we not?

I hear the report of a double-barrelled gun.
The doe in heat has called.
My heart cannot sleep
as I lie here alone.

Yet I must forget the sound of those guns.
Night talks about other things on campbeds,
of them, whose double-barrelled guns killed the deer tonight,
on whose dinner plates satisfaction was served,
the taste of deer flesh and bone.
They too are like you.
Their hearts too are withering away on their campbeds,
thinking, just thinking.

This pain, this love is everywhere,
in the locust, in the worm, in the breasts of men,
in all our lives.
We are all
like those slain deer in spring moonlight.

Translated from Bengali by Clinton B. Seely

Bhanuji Rao (*b.* 1926)

Fish

Dawn,
like petals of drenched roses.
Six naked bodies
glide forward furtively
in the practised motions of some dance,
rippling the water's sleek body.

Slowly they close in on one another,
cutting across the cries
of kingfisher and kite.
They move up, six torsos,
black and naked,
deepening the repose of snail and ancient toad.

And now the net is wound,
rising up
under twelve greedy, watchful eyes;
threshing bodies of carp and tiny fry,
brilliant as the sun.

Translated from Oriya by Jayanta Mahapatra

Bishnu De (*b.* 1909)

Santhal Poems, 1

We cut grass,
we keep cutting grass
on the big hill.
My throat's tired and parched,
I can't bear it, my love,
take me to the stream by the tamarind tree.

There are leeches by the stream
under the tamarind tree,
let's not go there.
My throat's hurting, my love,
take me to the stream
by the mango tree.

The boys have left their cows
by the stream near the mango grove
and gone off to dance.
Let's go to the riverbank, my love,

where you'll cup your hands
and let me drink my fill.

Translated from Bengali by Samir Dasgupta
and Stephen N. Hay

Nida Fazli (*b.* 1940)

A Page from the New Diary

The day changed
only on the paper calendar;
the steel-belted dial of time
turned,
the clockwork doll
stepped beyond the threshold
of its home
and danced in circles.
Hands clapped,
laughter crowned the scene.
A playful sun-deer
panted and trembled,
dashed into the black tyre
of the last bus,
fell, and went to pieces.
One more day
turned away offended.
Exactly
what I had feared
happened today.
Today, again,
nothing happened.

Translated from Urdu by Baidar Bakht
and Leslie Lavigne

Atmanam

Next Page

                    me on the floor
                            lizard on the wall
                    swaying shadows
                            from the hanging lamp
                    fading voices
                            from nightfall
                    a child crying
                            in the distance
                    a leaky tap
                            heard in the dark
                    silkmoths flying zigzag
                            in the windy room
                    a laughing *kolam*
                            design of dots
                    floating in the sky
                            in the thick of night
                    that hugs you in the fraction
                            of a second
                    in the middle of this swirl
                            of space
                    a lizard on the floor
                            me on the wall

                    Translated from Tamil by A.K. Ramanujan

Ravji Patel (1939–68)

Whirlwind

                    When I'd finished my bath
                    I wiped my body
                    with the smell of the green fields.

The moment I whistled
cows jumped in
through the window,
carrying the morning's sunshine
on their horns;

buffaloes jumped in,
their bodies slick
with the waters of the lake
foul with fish-smells;

goats jumped in,
with lonely roads,
the muddy edges of roads,
deserted fields,
and peacock feathers
in their eyes;

I jumped in,
a whirlwind in the house.

Translated from Gujarati by Hansa Jhaveri

N. Pichamurti (1900–78)

National Bird

Having spelt it out in blood
they were determined
to rouse the nation,
to put an end
to the oppression and bungling.
When they went to the forest
once, for game,
a hyena ran into them,
rolled its eyes and laughed;
a black bear rose before them
like a storm;
a viper, a whip-snake and a python,

their mouths close to the ground,
fed themselves without stirring;
a lion's tumultuous roar
shattered to bits the four corners of the world.
Returning, they staggered along,
hands trembling, legs faltering;
saw peacocks and were thrilled.
Thinking, 'Begging is pointless, one must trespass;
it's no good asking, one must grab,'
a few plucked the tail
with its thousand eyes,
and returned overjoyed,
shooing off, with feathers,
poverty, disease, sorcery, witchcraft,
exclaiming, 'Begone, go away.'
Others pulled out its tongue,
thinking it was a specific.
And still others thought,
'The peacock's neck is ours,'
broke it off and hurried away.
The rest tore its body to shreds,
claiming, 'It's ours, too,'
roasted and ate it.
As they turned homewards,
hunger assuaged,
the inarticulate land
groaned aloud.

Translated from Tamil by R. Parthasarathy

K.V. Tirumalesh (*b.* 1940)

Face to Face

1

A fat cat came into my drawing room,
looked at me and stopped short.
Perhaps it didn't expect me there.

Certainly not on a Monday afternoon
when everyone's at the office.
It looked at me reproachfully. Our eyes met,
in an undeclared war
on who should turn away first.
I didn't know a cat's eye
could be so still.

2

Stiff tail lifted, back hair bristling,
claws drawn in—
all in all, the cat was tight as a bow
and occupied my entire field of vision,
as if I had lost my way,
had fallen on prehistoric continents,
on unknown seas.
But I didn't blink an eyelid.
The cat didn't blink an eyelid either.
In a special state basic to man and beast,
the cat stood, all cat, in front of me.
I didn't know a cat's eyes
could be such orphans.

3

In the end, it was the beast that lost.
At least I thought so.
The stiff body relaxed slowly,
the cat slinked away like a cat.
My field of vision suddenly empty,
it occurred to me—
I could have accepted the cat's respect
for its cat-self.
What did I gain after all?
One should win like Bahubali—
by yielding, by giving up.
I didn't know a cat's eyes
could contain so much grief.

Translated from Kannada by A.K. Ramanujan

Buddhadeva Bose (1908–74)

Frogs

The rains have come, the frogs are bursting with joy.
They're singing in chorus, in loud jubilant voices.

Nothing to fear today: no drought, no shortage of worms,
No snakes' jaws, no stones thrown by mischievous boys.

Cloud-like the grasses thicken: in the fields the lush waters stand.
Louder and louder leaps their brief hour of immortality.

They have no necks, but their throats are rich and swollen;
And what sleek bodies, what cold gem-like eyes!

Eyes staring upwards, fixed in meditation,
Ecstatic, lidless, like the eyes of *rishis* gazing on God.

The rain has stopped; the shadows slant.
Their songs float like hymns on the slow, attentive air.

Now the day dies in silence; but a sombre drone
Pierces the twilight; the thin sky leans down to listen.

Darkness and rain: and we're warm in bed.
But one unwearied phrase enters our sleep—

The final *shloka* of their mystic chanting,
The croak, croak, croak of the last fanatic frog.

Translated from Bengali by the poet

Sarveshwar Dayal Saxena (1927–84)

The Black Panther

1

The black panther is sleeping on the crags;
the colour of the crags is black.

The black panther
is stretching and yawning on the crags;
the colour of the crags is changing.

The black panther
is racing over the crags;
the colour of the crags has changed.

The black panther
is mauling his prey on the crags;
the crags are no longer crags,
they've changed into panthers.

A single panther is changing
the whole jungle
into a black panther.

2

In the twilight at dusk,
having killed his prey,
the black panther
drinks water
at the red, stony river.

This river
is his past,
is his present,
is his future.

For centuries,
with this river's help,
the black panther has changed
into the black jungle's throbbing.

Translated from Hindi by Vinay Dharwadker

VII. The Possessed City

Adil Jussawalla (*b.* 1940)

Sea Breeze, Bombay

> Partition's people stitched
> Shrouds from a flag, gentlemen scissored Sind.
> An opened people, fraying across the cut
> > Country, reknotted themselves on this island.
>
> > Surrogate city of banks,
> Brokering and bays, refugees' harbour and port,
> Gatherer of ends whose brick beginnings work
> > Loose like a skin, spotting the coast,
>
> > Restore us to fire. New refugees,
> Wearing blood-red wool in the worst heat,
> Come from Tibet, scanning the sea from the north,
> > Dazed, holes in their cracked feet.
>
> > Restore us to fire. Still,
> Communities tear and re-form; and still, a breeze,
> Cooling our garrulous evenings, investigates nothing,
> > Ruffles no tempers, uncovers no root,
>
> And settles no one adrift of the mainland's histories.

Sunil Gangopadhyay (*b.* 1934)

Calcutta and I

Calcutta sits like a stone on my chest.
I must destroy her before I go—
lure her away to Haldia port,
feed her shredded-coconut sweets poisoned with rat poison
—Calcutta sits like a stone on my chest.
Calcutta forges the moon's own light,
she has learnt how to adulterate her kisses

with ground pebbles and mashed thorns.
She forgets to add sugar to her tea, which is like tears,
and she has so many admirers
that even during the day, even at noon,
she lies with her thighs open, ready to receive them.

How can I let you go without any fuss,
my beautiful one, to the Supreme Court at Delhi?
I'll wear a fragrance on my heart
and cling to your arms in acute need
as we go for a drive in a taxi some evening.
You'll twist to the band at a restaurant,
let your sari slip off your shoulders
and hold up the two cameras of your breasts
—much to the relish of Jadu, Madhu, and Shyam.
With your body emanating such music
you're like the precious light in a mirror.
I could bring a completely poetic tribute
from the city's southern quarters
and lay it at your feet. Shall I also bring
on a golden tray a lotus which your hands can carry?
You'll be murdered at midnight.

How can you evade my clutches, Calcutta?
You can't hide in Canning Street—
even if you flee down the sidestreets of Chinatown.
I'll chase you like a tiger
leaping over the traffic lights
of miserable Barabazar.
My pursuit will reach out across Chowringhee
like a convalescent's diet. My painful love
will change into an airborne phantom without supports
to seek revenge—where will you hide?
I'll turn around all the steamers on the Ganga
and switch on a gigantic searchlight
and look for you in the dark maidan
and grab you by the throat.

I'll secretly pour explosives
down all the ducts branching through your body,

then light a match under your loins—
whole rows of mansions will be hurled into the air,
brick and wood will fly in all directions,
all the love-making, the ornaments,
the whole immortal universe of Chitpore,
everything will be blown up in an instant.

When you pushed me nearer death,
didn't you know that nothing could save you
from our ritual dying together?

Translated from Bengali by Sujit Mukherjee
and Meenakshi Mukherjee

Sunanda Tripathy (*b.* 1964)

Tryst

When the whole city is asleep
I take off my anklets
and come into your room
with soft, stolen steps.
You lie there, unmoving
on the disordered bed,
books strewn all around.
In their midst, alone, you lie asleep,
the smile of some strange contentment
on your face.
I sit quietly by the bed,
smoothe your dishevelled hair,
then bend down and with my sharp nails
tear open your chest,
and with both my hands scoop out
a fistful of pulsating soft pink flesh.

I'm spellbound by the odour of the flesh,
I hold it to my breast.
For a moment
word and silence become one—
then sky and earth
become one.

Before you come awake
I put the flesh back in its place,
caress your open chest.
The wound fills up in a moment
as if nothing had happened.

As before, you go on sleeping,
and I walk quietly from your room.

Translated from Oriya by J.P. Das and Arlene Zide

Vinay Dharwadker (*b.* 1954)

New Delhi, 1974

The city has spread quietly, suddenly. Everywhere
it springs up, this futile architecture, its garish forms

shuffled and heaped, its grass sprouting sparse
and indifferent, its women brittle with paint,

its wrists young and hairless, dipped into the pool
where gold reflections rise, quiver at the rims of its eyes.

The old scalps are dry, each hair has lost its root,
and the mouth that rehearsed its verses in these streets

now is elsewhere. The monuments are black, rainblack
and shoulderless, and the plains that once stretched

green towards the south are grey with dust and grime.
The old have nowhere to go now, in this new

city they haven't built, and the impatient young
are idle, and don't know where to turn.

Dhoomil (1935–75)

The City, Evening, and an Old Man: Me

I've taken the last drag
and stubbed out my cigarette in the ashtray,
and now I'm a respectable man
with all the trappings of civility.

When I'm on vacation
I don't hate anyone.
I don't have any protest march to join.
I've drunk all the liquor
in the bottle marked
FOR DEFENCE SERVICES ONLY
and thrown it away in the bathroom.
That's the sum total of my life.
(Like every good citizen
I draw the curtains across my windows
the moment I hear the air-raid siren.
These days it isn't the light outside
but the light inside that's dangerous.)

I haven't done a thing to deserve
a statue whose unveiling
would make the wise men of this city
waste a whole busy day.
I've been sitting in a corner of my dinner plate
and leading a very ordinary life.

What I inherited were citizenship
in the neighbourhood of a jail
and gentlemanliness
in front of a slaughter-house.
I've tied them both to my own convenience
and taken them two steps forward.
The municipal government has taught me
to stay on the left side of the road.

(To succeed in life you don't need
to read Dale Carnegie's book
but to understand traffic signs.)

Other than petty lies
I don't know the weight of a gun.
On the face of the traffic policeman
doing his drill in the square
I've always seen the map of democracy.

And now I don't have a single worry,
I don't have to do a thing.
I've reached the stage in life
when files begin to close.
I'm sitting in my own chair on the verandah
without any qualms.
The sun's setting on the toe of my shoe.
A bugle's blowing in the distance.
This is the time when the soldiers come back,
and the possessed city
is now slowly turning its madness
into windowpanes and lights.

Translated from Hindi by Vinay Dharwadker

Naresh Guha (*b.* 1924)

Winding Sand

> There are many winding rivers
> Which I have changed to sand
> Since the time when,
> Through a story's black hair,
> The vague heart of my childhood
> Crossed a courtyard
> Patterned by moonlight hours.
> She stands there with lowered eyes
> At the window on the upper floor.

I turn on the blue light
After the evening's shower of rain.
She shuts the window.
A train passes in the distance.
It is rumoured that Tapati Sen
Will soon be married.

The shimmering lake
In the shadow of the pines
Quivers in the breeze
Of the pale moonlit evening.
Finesse is still needed.
Who is coming? Who comes
With light feet over the grass?

No one. I realize my mistake.
The monotonous night
Comes and goes.
(What hand do I have
In the shaping of life?)

Cigarettes and women's bodies
Flare and burn out in the camp
In the city, in the village.
In the small hours of the morning
The rain falls
On roofs, on roads,
On streetcorners in the metropolis.

Translated from Bengali by Lila Ray

Ghulam Mohammed Sheikh (*b*. 1937)

Jaisalmer, 1

In a desert land, this pearl-studded city.
Peacocks perch on the brackets
and elephants roam on the walls.
Every balcony lace-embroidered in stone,
every window festooned
with the gashes of blunt swords.
In the twilight, walls flare like orange *odhnis*.
Eight generations of hands
have smoothed the door's iron ring.
Black goats loiter in the courtyard;
beyond the yard door, the dutiful camel neighs.
Red garments dry on the middle wall.
A limp flame flickers
in the room's mouldy darkness.
In the hearth's red flush,
in the *chundadi*'s glow,
a golden girl kneads a loafshaped city.

Translated from Gujarati by Saleem Peeradina
and the poet

R. Parthasarathy (*b*. 1934)

Speaking of Places

1

I cannot stop thinking of Srirangam:
I roll the name on the tongue
for comfort. I know, one day

I shall arrive there.
Her towers, a constellation
of beryl, pearl and coral.

Didn't the Romans long ago travel this way?
I step into the waters of the Kaveri,
turn its diamond in my palm.

Praise Ranganatha on his serpent bed.
Every island swells towards Srirangam.
Every river floods the Kaveri.

Again and again my lips cup
the golden bowl, poetry
scooped out of the ordinary air

with the prayer: 'Burn the sin of pride
from my forehead. Let me abide,
Lord of the Island, in Srirangam.'

2

Her rivers draw my breath:
they are my refuge
in this world. Everywhere temples

splash in the morning, the hymn
of Shankara fluting in their ears:
bhaja govindam bhaja govindam. . . .

The torch of death unextinguished
burns forever. The ghats explode,
pullulate, with flesh.

Siva descends from Kailasa:
on the chessboard that is Kashi
throws skulls for dice.

Unmoved, Parvati watches.
Her breasts glow with the bronze of passion,
obscure a thousand bells.

Here, prayer and desire are the two faces
of every hole-in-the-pocket coin
that sticks to the river's bowl.

What is it about the earth
of India that consents
to be shaped into a poem?

Sumitranandan Pant (1900–77)

Almora Spring

Coral and emerald shade,
sun's heat first gold then silver;
snow mountain scent on silken breezes,
a hundred jewelled birds painting the sky.
On autumn's brittle yellow bodies
a world of newborn beauty budding,
while blaze of coolest green
sheds everywhere its tender light.
New heaven of pleasure, youth and love,
and loveliness created afresh;
Nature's in bud, horizon blossoms,
skies rain bird-song and hum of bees.
—See, like a bright cicada spreading its wings
about to fly to flowering valleys—
this is the Almora spring,
blossoming on every mountainside.

Translated from Hindi by David Rubin

Shamsher Bahadur Singh (1911–93)

On the Slope of this Hill

On the rocky grassy slope of this hill, Topsy and I.
The quick breathing of the spaniel sitting alertly beside me.
A half-finished, distracted sketch;
Open in my lap, a notebook, bright white in the sun.
Standing all around me, big and small trees, stirring, glistening,
     very green.
Rainclouds—radiant with sunshine, radiant in the blue sky,
     the washed sky.
Like big and small puffs of cotton scattered everywhere.
Sometimes the resonance of a clean gentle sweet wind.
The background behind the mild, mellow whirring and droning
     on the hill, in the woods, on the slope—a railway station.

The clanking, hissing, groaning of engines: their long
     exhalations
—when this wasn't here, there was only the soft and sweet
     music of the wind.

. . . A low-then-loud-once-or-twice-shrill whistle. An engine
     shunting—
The mixed-up whispers of the winds among themselves. Wide-
     awake Topsy.
Below, in the distance, like a huge, smoky-green, shimmering
     garden, with some of its countless roofs shining here and
     there, the city of Jabalpur.

Its green lawns, and in scattered places, its green compounds.
And below us, close at hand, the red-and-black stony mounds
     of dug-up earth.
. . . A noise—what bird was that?
                              again? again?

That glass-house nearby. Somewhere also something like a
     children's quarrel.
Little groups of women-workers carrying loads of red mud on
     their heads.

The breathing of an engine letting off its steam as it draws
    closer slowly—
Then quickly; the exhalations dying down one by one: but no
    —suddenly, a long whistle.
The sharp slanting slope of sunshine.

Translated from Hindi by Vinay Dharwadker

Umashankar Joshi (*b.* 1911)

Passing through Rajasthan

My eyes fly out of the window.
What space!
' . . . Friend, take a seat, anywhere you like. . . .
Comfortable?'
Gada-gada-gada-gada,
The train moves on, moves on.
My eyes rush out of the window,
They escape and wander.

My mind becomes a desert;
My thoughts, like sheep, root out and champ
The grass that may or may not be there.

There, a hill lifts its head;
My mind leans to rest on it,
Climbs along the trails on its crest,
And flutters with the temple flag.

' . . . Watch out! The water's spilt. Mind your luggage!
The clay jar's broken. . . . '
For me, a vision of water
in the middle of the desert.
Gada-gada-gada-gada,
The train moves on, moves on.

Water? Not here, but in the deepest well,
Or there, in the sky,
Or there, where that fort stands
On walls of rock,
As if the dry land had raised its fist.
Surely that's a sign for water.

Look, there,
Above the dome,
Padmini stands gloriously
On the evening's flaming pyre,
Looking at the fire
That shoots up from the heart of eternity.

Evening disappears.
Through the desert darkness
This train plunges on, a streak of light,
As though a camel pulls a plough
Moment by moment.
At every gash of the blade,
Earth turns on her side.
Night comes spreading out the stars.
Let's see what harvest God will reap.
Gada-gada-gada-gada,
The train moves on, moves on.

Translated from Gujarati by Niranjan Bhagat
and Carlo Coppola

Chemmanam Chacko (*b.* 1926)

Rice

I

I come home at the end of four years of research
in North India, having earned a doctoral degree
and generous praise for my work on making toys with husk;
bored with eating chapaties day after day,
I'm eager to eat a meal of *athikira* rice.

It will be the planting season when I get there,
and my father—his handloom dhoti stained with yellow mud,
excited about the waters of the Varanganal canal—
will greet me from the fields below our house,
amidst the shouts of ploughing with several oxen.

The oxen will stop when they see me
walking with my suitcase, and my father,
without smiling the smile slowly forming on his lips,
will call from the field: 'And when did you start from there?'

My little brother, carrying the tender saplings
to be planted in the field where the ploughing is done,
will run when he sees me, and call out loud
within earshot of the house: 'Mother, brother's arrived!'

Walking cautiously along the dyke
so as not to upset the baskets full of seed,
I'll reach home in good time, at last,
just as my mother drains the well-cooked rice.
O train, will you run a little faster—
let me get home quickly and eat my fill.

II

The bus stops on the road across from the house.
When I left this place, palm-thatched houses could be seen
in the distance on the right—but now there's nothing,
except for trees. How the place has changed!

Rubber plants, twice my height,
now stand in rows around me on the ridge
where *modan* and *vellaran* used to be sown,
and confuse my path as I walk home.

There's no bustle of men below,
no shouts of ploughing; and when I look,
the whole field is planted over with arecanut palms,
and in the corner, along the canal, stand the dealwood trees.

I enter the house. Beyond the southern wing,
my father's watching them fix up the machine
for making rubber sheets—how happy
and contented the look on his face!

My father says, with obvious pride:
'Son, we've stopped working on all the rice.
It was quite inconvenient. The farmer gained nothing—
only fools turn to rice-farming for gain.
This is better money—what good times!
The government gives rice to those who don't have paddy fields.'

My little brother runs in to meet me—
I, eager to have a full meal of *athikira* rice.
He's carrying the rations for the whole household—
he trips over something and scatters the wheat all over the yard.

Above us, a 'ship of the sky' roars northwards,
drowning my brother's loud cries—
the Chief Minister's off like an arrow to the Centre
to clamour for more grains, now flying high
above the cash crops, now growing tall like the trees,
since no one here promotes the farming of rice.

Can we get some husk from the Centre, too,
to make toys with it? I don't know.

Translated from Malayalam by K. Ayyappa Paniker

Keki N. Daruwalla (*b.* 1937)

Of Mohenjo Daro at Oxford

He was digging; his fingers
had worked through the ravelled mittens
so that I noticed
the green crescent of his thumbnail.
Gladiolus bulbs
lay in a fibrous heap around him.
He wanted them out
before the winter got them.
Behind him, as the sun
came out for an instant,
the Cotswolds flashed an after-rain smile
and rooks swung high.
'They nested here once,'
he said, pointing
to the bowering elms across the road,
'before the traffic flushed them out.'

He took me in for lunch,
a salad and a casserole
washed down with ale.
It was when pouring coffee
that I asked, 'When will you talk
of Mohenjo Daro?'
His lips cracked, his dentures smiled
and the light glowed in his pupils.
'What is there to say
except that I was there
when the first ceramic shards came out
and the terra-cotta figurines.
The thrill of the first seal,
the humped bull standing majestic,
with his dewlap like a sail unfurled.

'They flourished for a thousand years
and when the bed of the river rose
their cities rose with it,
the ground-plan never changing.
Nine strata of the city we shovelled off,
skinning the onion layers
where pasts had settled over earlier pasts.

'A Gilgamesh motif on a seal,
a man fighting two tigers,
sent me voyaging to Sumer,
argosies sailing up the Tigris
laden with Indian cotton;
a turquoise bead, a lapis lazuli trinket
brought caravans from Tabriz and Shraz,
the harness-bells jangling, dogs barking
as the centuries waved to each other
on the crossroads.

'Glinting out of the rubble
a copper axe with a shaft-hole
cried out to me,
superior to anything the Indus people made—
their axe heads lashed to handles
had no chance against the invaders.
An Armenoid skull told me where he came from
and the street rang with his war-cries.

'There are evenings my house is unlit.
I sit watching the rooks settling into the trees,
and cars scream past on the M-40.
Headlights vault in through windows,
shadows clean the wall and sail away.
A wind of reflections rustles the curtains
as I think of the Indus people.
For a thousand years the brewery of life
fermented and stank there, seething in the vats.
Passions worked themselves out,
seasons and festivals went round
like bullocks on a threshing floor.

They were a happy people, even their bondmen
had brick cottages with two rooms.
Then like a geological shift
a people came from the north,
and I came upon a hearth
with cold cinders, four thousand years old.

'Why didn't I write about all this?
That's a good question.
But Tutenkhamen was the rage then,
the Pharaoh's gold-mask and the Pharaoh's curse.
Who cared about the Indus then?
Now it is too late;
I search for memories,
they have swung away like the rooks.
I dig for words
and I can't find them.'

Amiya Chakravarty (1901–86)

Fire

Writing verse on smooth paper with a new Parker pen
is utterly American. Some sunlight outside the window,
shaded blue curtains, books on a shelf close at hand
(Huxley's latest prose, a sea-story by Hemingway
to be read at leisure), some cello records left behind
by a friend. A melody of trembling peace haunts the mind,
all distant thoughts were drowned in the lake on the way home,
there's just a chance that the Korean war might end.

Line after line of mere words flowing from the pen!
I close my notebook. The sunlight flashes again,
and the blue emptiness of the curtains, the muted print
of books (shining prose, a deceptive commentary;
the stormy yarn of an old man fighting a whale).

The invisible Spanish strings sound faintly again,
then the fullness of words, drowsing in poetry,
and the lake's glimmer. But Korea is on fire,
and the radio transmits the flames in waves.

Translated from Bengali by Sujit Mukherjee

B.C. Ramachandra Sharma (*b.* 1925)

American Tourist

Stupid of me to think you were salmon
flapping your fins to swim upstream.
You didn't catch the jet to London
to lay eggs. Insemination was your dream.

Your eyelids are shutters, they take quick snaps
by day, and timed exposures by night;
your walk is an arrow in flight;
your questions drip-drop from a leaky tap.

The fish is different: a flying arc, it dives
only to rise and float away,
writing its story as it moves
with no care for what's beyond its snout.

Its essence is silence before, and after,
the net drains it out of the water.
No force drives it to its source
as you're driven. Its life is water on its course.

Translated from Kannada by A.K. Ramanujan,
using the poet's own English version

Shiv K. Kumar (*b.* 1921)

Days in New York

Here I live in a garbage can.
The pile grows bigger each week
with the broken homes
splintered all around.
A black cat chases a shadow
down the passageway:
its whiskers presage another snowstorm.

The white of the negro maid's eyeballs
is the only clean thing here,
besides, of course, the quart gallon of milk
squatting at my door.
They won't believe it here
that Ganges water can work miracles:
in spite of the cartloads
of dead men's ashes and bones—
daily offerings to the river.

I open each morning my neighbour's Times,
whisked away from his door
before he stirs.
Gloved hands leave no fingerprints.
And a brisk review of all our yesterdays is no sin.

En route to perdition
I sometimes stop at Grand Central to piss.
Where else can one ease one's nerves
when the bladder fills up
like a child's balloon?
In the Gents, each in his stall,
we stand reduced to the thing itself.
Questions catapult in the air:
'Are you a Puerto Rican?
A Jamaican? A Red Indian?'
I look for the feathers on my skull,

a band around my forehead.
And mumble, 'No, a brown Indian,
from the land of Gandhi.'
The stranger briskly zips his soul
and vanishes past the shoeblack,
who turns to shine a lanky New Yorker
swaddled in the high chair like Lincoln.
Incidentally, there are no beggars at Grand Central.
Only eyes, eyes, eyes,
staring at lamp-posts.
Back in my den after dusk
I bandaid the day's bruises.
Outside the window perches the grey sky,
an ominous bird wrapped in nuclear fog.

At night the Voices of America
break in upon my tenuous frequency,
intoning the same fact three times,
till the sediment grips the Hudson's soul.
But my soul is still my own.
For, every Sunday morning, I descend
into purgatory,
the basement where three laundromats
gulp down nickels,
to wash all our sins.
But the brown of my skin defies
all bleachers.
How long will this eclipse last?

VIII. Do Something, Brother

Kunwar Narain (b. 1927)

Towards Delhi

I've seen him many times before
go dragging along in the direction
in which the horsemen are headed.

Both hands tied, in helplessness, once more
who was he? I can't say
because only two tied hands
reached Delhi.

*Translated from Hindi by Vinay Dharwadker
and Aparna Dharwadker*

Narayan Surve (b. 1926)

Lifetime

A whole lifetime assigned to me:
even the light when I was born
was assigned to me;
I said the things I was assigned to say.
Cursing under my breath,
I walked the street assigned to me;
I came back to the room
assigned to me;
I lived the life I was assigned to live.
They say we go to heaven
if we follow the path assigned to us.
Between the four pillars assigned to us
I spit:
                there.

Translated from Marathi by Vinay Dharwadker

Namdeo Dhasal (b. 1949)

Stone-masons, My Father, and Me

> Stone-masons give stones dreams to dream;
> I set a match to fireworks.
> > They say one mustn't step into
> > one's father's life:
> > > I do; I scratch
> > his elbows,
> > > his armpits.
>
> Stone-masons give stones flowers;
> I play horns and trumpets.
> > I overtake the Parsi who stands
> > turned to stone
> > > by the bodies of four women
> > bent like bows.
> I see my father's bloodied rump.
> > In the chaos of the dark
> > I smoke a cheroot
> > > and smoulder with memories
> > till my lips get burnt.
>
> Stone-masons inseminate stones;
> I count exhausted horses.
> > I harness myself to a cart;
> > I handle
> > my father's corpse;
> > > I burn.
>
> Stone-masons mix blood with stones;
> I carry a load of stones.
> > Stone-masons build
> > a stone house.
> > I break heads with stones.

Translated from Marathi by Vinay Dharwadker

Dom Moraes (*b.* 1938)

Babur

By night, Tingribirdi, the hills burned
In loops and whorls of twined fire,
Arabesques of fire in the forest
And in the valleys pools of fire.
Over and under me, liquid fire
Poured itself into all crevices,
Reddening the rocks, the fox's earth.
Embered nests were empty, the birds departed.

The tribesmen did this in peace,
Etching their fields from the ash left.
I know war, but no taken town,
Spired in flames, ever seized my eye,
Tingribirdi, like that land on fire.
Those forests, stroked by the purest element
Were turned to ashes to make life.
I have made ashes, but for death.

Miles from that place, we camped.
Reeds and a river: mosquitoes
Came at nightfall with the lamps.
The opium confection, then wine.
I heard music and I slept,
Pyramids of heads on my pillow,
Soundless flames round my flesh,
Faces, whispers, omens.

The dead in the dust.
Familiars of the field, vultures
Alighted as angels on each corpse.
One, in that sleeping, seemed my son.
With a great cry I drove them away,
Awoke weeping, ate opium confection:
Drowsy afterwards, saw myself
As I am, lonely in all lands.

Now on the way to another war
I have seated myself beside the river.
Far from sweet melons and the snow
I arrange these words for you, Tingribirdi.
I have little time left for words.
My hard men fasten their helmets.
The ponies whinny in their hobbles.
Drums for departure scare the crows.

Grey burnish shows in a crow's feathers
As though He first meant to make a dove.
I wrought words before I fought wars,
Steel in those words like swords
Hurt me also: my books are where I bled,
As when they drove me out to the badlands,
Wifeless, to echo the cry of the wolf.
Then betrayals by friends: the death of friends.

In the flames always with me
I will not burn: like a plainsman's ox
I return to the yoke of those years,
Who was healer and killer in the hills!
If you look for me, I am not here.
My writings will tell you where I am.
Tingribirdi, they point out my life like
Lines drawn in the map of my palm.

Jagannath Prasad Das (b. 1936)

The Corpse

Someone's lifeless body lies in the street
surrounded by people.
Many simply walk past,
others cannot bear to look at it;
one man's step falters, another falls silent,
and another shuts his eyes at the sight.

One passes by reciting mantras along the street;
for whom did this child pluck flowers?
Who laughed here,
who stretched out his arms
to put a halt to time,
and whose screams are lost
in the deserted street?

In the light's rush upstream,
someone was lost on the way;
the heart's many dreams were ground to ash.
Someone sighs deeply,
Someone measures life
with a burning candle,
and another finds his own way
in the half-light.

The people have all gone away;
the street is deserted, laughter extinguished
in the endlessness of space.
The corpse lies in the middle of the street.

And I lie fast asleep on a lonely island.

Translated from Oriya by Jayanta Mahapatra

Sati Kumar (*b.* 1938)

Come Back, Alexander

> The famished plain
> spread before my eyes
> screamed again, 'Come back, Alexander!'
>
> Every invader is red
> and, with him, the cloud of dust is red.
> There's no water in it.

The cloud of dust
has only a famished plain
always screaming, 'Come back, Alexander!'

Translated from Punjabi by Manohar Bandopadhyay

Agyeya (1911–86)

Hiroshima

On this day, the sun
Appeared—no, not slowly over the horizon—
But right in the city square.
A blast of dazzle poured over,
Not from the middle sky,
But from the earth torn raggedly open.

Human shadows, dazed and lost, pitched
In every direction: this blaze,
Not risen from the east,
Smashed in the city's heart—
An immense wheel
Of Death's swart suncar, spinning down and apart
In every direction.

Instant of a sun's rise and set.
Vision-annihilating flare one compressed noon.

And then?
It was not human shadows that lengthened, paled, and died;
It was men suddenly become as mist, then gone.
The shadows stay:
Burned on rocks, stones of these vacant streets.

A sun conjured by men converted men to air, to nothing;
White shadows singed on the black rock give back
Man's witness to himself.

Translated from Hindi by the poet and Leonard Nathan

Vikram Seth (*b.* 1952)

A Doctor's Journal Entry for August 6, 1945

The morning stretched calm, beautiful, and warm.
Sprawling half-clad, I gazed out at the form
Of shimmering leaves and shadows. Suddenly
A strong flash, then another, startled me.
I saw the old stone lantern brightly lit.
Magnesium flares? While I debated it,
The roof, the walls and, as it seemed, the world
Collapsed in timber and debris, dust swirled
Around me—in the garden now—and, weird,
My drawers and undershirt disappeared.
A splinter jutted from my mangled thigh.
My right side bled, my cheek was torn, and I
Dislodged, detachedly, a piece of glass,
All the time wondering what had come to pass.
Where was my wife? Alarmed, I gave a shout,
'Where are you, Yecko-san?' My blood gushed out.
The artery in my neck? Scared for my life,
I called out, panic-stricken, to my wife.
Pale, bloodstained, frightened, Yecko-san emerged,
Holding her elbow. 'We'll be fine,' I urged—
'Let's get out quickly.' Stumbling to the street
We fell, tripped up by something at our feet.
I gasped out, when I saw it was a head:
'Excuse me, please excuse me—' He was dead:
A gate had crushed him. There we stood, afraid.
A house standing before us tilted, swayed,
Toppled, and crashed. Fire sprang up in the dust,
Spread by the wind. It dawned on us we must
Get to the hospital: we needed aid—
And I should help my staff too. (Though this made
Sense to me then, I wonder how I could
Have hoped, hurt as I was, to do much good.)
My legs gave way. I sat down on the ground.
Thirst seized me, but no water could be found.

My breath was short, but bit by bit my strength
Seemed to revive, and I got up at length.
I was still naked, but I felt no shame.
This thought disturbed me somewhat, till I came
Upon a soldier, standing silently,
Who gave the towel round his neck to me.
My legs, stiff with dried blood, rebelled. I said
To Yecko-san she must go on ahead.
She did not wish to, but in our distress
What choice had we? A dreadful loneliness
Came over me when she had gone. My mind
Ran at high speed, my body crept behind.
I saw the shadowy forms of people, some
Were ghosts, some scarecrows, all were wordless, dumb—
Arms stretched straight out, shoulder to dangling hand;
It took some time for me to understand
The friction on their burns caused so much pain
They feared to chafe flesh against flesh again.
Those who could, shuffled in a blank parade
Towards the hospital. I saw, dismayed,
A woman with a child stand in my path—
Both naked. Had they come back from the bath?
I turned my gaze, but I was at a loss
That she should stand thus, till I came across
A naked man—and now the thought arose
That some strange thing had stripped us of our clothes.
The face of an old woman on the ground
Was marred with suffering, but she made no sound.
Silence was common to us all. I heard
No cries of anguish, or a single word.

K. Nisar Ahmad (*b. 1936*)

America, America

Whenever your American Way of Life is raised to the sky,
I feel like pulling off one by one you folks' ties, suits, skirts,
lifting from the blood-baths the Spaniards, the Germans,
the Portuguese, the Englishmen, the Negroes,
the pirates, the killers, the adulteresses,
and throwing them at you and laughing aloud—
but I see Lincoln, Kennedy, King,
and I stutter, stumble, bow my head, and keep quiet.

Whenever, in the name of stamping out Communists and Nazis,
you fuck up people's lives and brag about it in *Life, Time,*
      etcetera,
I want to spit on you, drink vodka,
and talk to Castro, De Gaulle, Ho Chi Minh, and Nasser—
but the Chinese and Pakistani invasions stab my memory,
and I see your hand of friendship, terrifying
and six thousand miles long,
and I shut my mouth.

When you fly flags of culture on the Empire State Building,
I see the male macho eyes in nightclubs and on the beaches,
      the 007s,
the Hollywood beat, the twist, the mental somersaults,
hashish, marijuana, LSD, the condoms, the perverse itches,
the mafiosos, the divorces at the rate of twenty-five a minute,
and I want to crow, clap my hands,
and broadcast it all to the world.
Lady Liberty faces the world and keeps her back to you—
I'd turn her around so that she can face your heart's slums,
      the black Harlems—
I'd snatch away the toy guns you give your children as birthday
      gifts,
and give them Bibles, Gitas, and Korans instead—
I'd like to give the lustre of Eastern sages

to your folks' pale morning-after bedsheet faces—
I'd like to rub the Nehru rose on LBJ's lips
and iron out all the knit brows
and the lines on his forehead—

America, America,

whenever you brag about your power
I'd like to tweak your ears and tell you about
the victories of the young Vietcong
rubbing out armies like bedbugs,
the shame and defeat of your CIA
overturning governments and setting up Yes-Men,
and your ladders to the moon and the satellites
that fell into the sea.

But then I remember
your wheat loans, your PL480s,
and foreign policy seals my lips.
I stomach the fact
that there's no country quite like you,
that when an elephant falls
it's still taller than a horse.
So I sew up my lips, America,
and I bow to you.

Whenever I bitch about and resent
all that growth of yours
which devours me silently in the news,
our poverty
our overpopulation
our geography
stop my tongue
and teach me lessons in patience.

Translated from Kannada by A.K. Ramanujan

A. Jayaprabha (b. 1957)

Burn this Sari

When I see this end
of the sari
on my shoulder
I think of chastity
a log
hung from my neck

It doesn't let me
stand up straight
it presses my chest with its hands
bows me down
teaches me shame
and whirls around me
a certain bird-like confusion

It hypnotizes me
telling me, 'You,
you're a woman,'
makes me forget I'm human

It covers both my shoulders
with my own hands
and flutters
announcing, 'See, see
this woman! She's chaste!'

I feel like screaming, 'No, no,
I'm not,'
but my throat doesn't open
I'm defeated by this sari

It pulls me in like a mire
it throws me down
like a whirlwind

It's the blame
generations have laid on me
the unseen patriarchal hand

This sari is the white
shroud on the corpse
that's me in this culture
of loot and plunder

If I've to stop
being the walking dead
I've to burn
this sari first
just burn this sari

Translated from Telugu by V. Narayana Rao
and A.K. Ramanujan

Imtiaz Dharker (*b.* 1954)

Purdah, 1

One day they said
she was old enough to learn some shame.
She found it came quite naturally.

Purdah is a kind of safety.
The body finds a place to hide.
The cloth fans out against the skin
much like the earth that falls
on coffins after they put the dead men in.

People she has known
stand up, sit down as they have always done.
But they make different angles
in the light, their eyes aslant,
a little sly.

She half-remembers things
from someone else's life,
perhaps from yours, or mine—
carefully carrying what we do not own:
between the thighs, a sense of sin.

We sit still, letting the cloth grow
a little closer to our skin.
A light filters inward
through our bodies' walls.
Voices speak inside us,
echoing in the spaces we have just left.

She stands outside herself,
sometimes in all four corners of a room.
Wherever she goes, she is always
inching past herself,
as if she were a clod of earth,
and the roots as well,
scratching for a hold
between the first and second rib.

Passing constantly out of her own hands
into the corner of someone else's eyes . . .
while doors keep opening
inward and again
inward.

Jyoti Lanjewar (*b.* 1950)

I Never Saw You

> Ma
> I never saw you
> in a brand new silk sari
> bordered with gold

with a string of golden beads
at your throat
bangles and bracelets on your arms
rubber chappals on your feet
    Ma
I saw you . . .
working in a gang of workers
repairing roads
your bare feet burning
on the burning ground
your child in a bundle of cloth
hung on a thorny tree
while you carried canisters of tar
I saw you . . .
carrying baskets of earth
with rags wrapped around your feet
giving a sweaty kiss
to the naked child who ran to you
on pattering feet
while you slaved for a scheme
of guaranteed daily wages
I saw you . . .
dragging a chain of tears behind you
pacifying your belly
helping to build the dam at the lake
while your own lips were parched
tormented by thirst
I saw you . . .
carefully climbing the scaffolding
of a beautiful new house
your feet swollen with pregnancy
carrying loads
of cement and sand on your head
for the sake of your dream
of a four-walled house of your own
I saw you . . .
late in the evening
untying the little bundle you had made
with the free end of your sari

to bring home salt and cooking oil
putting a shiny five-paisa coin
in my tiny hand and saying
Go eat what you want
holding the baby in the cradle
to your breast and saying
Get educated like Ambedkar
let the basket of labour
fall from my hands
I saw you . . .
burning the sticks of your body
lighting a mass
of dry crushed sugarcane for fuel
in the stove
feeding everyone else four *bhakris*
and staying half-hungry yourself
saving only a small piece in your pouch
for later
I saw you . . .
washing and cleaning in four homes
saying no with dignity
to the leftovers offered there
covering yourself modestly
with the same tattered end of the sari
in which you made your countless little bundles
I saw you . . .
right in the middle of the town-square
roundly cursing
the mother and sister of any man
who dared to walk past you
with a lecherous gaze
I saw you . . .
walking through a crowd
with a basket-load of fruit
drawing the end of your sari over your head
picking up and raising your chappal
at anyone who pushed you around
I saw you . . .
at sunset

after you had carried
a mountain of work all day
your feet turning homeward and slicing
the darkness
angrily throwing out the man
who had come back drunk
I saw you . . .
on the Long March
striding in front
with your sari drawn tightly around you
shouting
We must change our name
bearing the blow
of a police baton on your arm
entering the jail
with your head held high
I saw you . . .
saying to your only son
who'd martyred himself in a police firing
You died for Bhima
your life became meaningful
telling the officer defiantly
that if you'd had two or three sons
you would've been more fortunate
you would've fought again
I saw you . . .
on your deathbed cot
counting your last moments
with a gift to charity
the money you had made and saved
by sifting through waste paper
I saw you . . .
saying
Live in unity
fight for Babasaheb
build a memorial to him
breathing your last with the words
Jai Bhima on your lips
I never saw you

praying with beads
for a brand new silk sari
   Ma
I saw you . . .

Translated from Marathi by Vinay Dharwadker

Ali Sardar Jafri (*b.* 1913)

Morsel

His mother weaves silk for a living,
his father spins cloth.
He left the womb's darkness
for a hovel's black heart.
When he leaves this place,
he'll become fodder for the mills.
To feed his innocent body,
he'll feed money's endless hunger.
His hands will squander flowers of gold.
His body will spend its silver.
His heart's blood will fuel the lamps
burning brightly in the windows of banks.
This child, small, innocent,
destined for capital's jaws,
stands asking mutely:
Can anyone save me?

Translated from Urdu by Kathleen Grant Jaeger
and Baidar Bakht

Sitakant Mahapatra (*b.* 1937)

The Election

Our jeep crawls to your village
seeking strange melodies
from the roaring sun:
'the common will'
from the criss-cross geometry
of private agonies.

Our dark longings don't touch you,
nor our trappings
of posters, symbols, speeches, handbills,
for your grief outlives empires.

The cold grandchildren
awaken in your heart
as you discern
muted allegories
on our ashen faces.

Here the great persuaders
are little things, and not so hidden:
cheap plastic, cheaper nylon,
dark glasses to blot out the sun.

With one foot in hunger
and the other in the soul,
you make your decision:
the anguish of choice.

Translated from Oriya by the poet

Subhash Mukhopadhyay (*b.* 1919)

The Task

I want these words
to stand.
I want these shadows
to see.
I want these scenes to move.

Don't call me
a poet.
I want to walk with the others
shoulder to shoulder
till I die.

So that in the end
I can put down my pen
beside the tractor
and say:
            Comrade,
give me a light.

Translated from Bengali by Pritish Nandy

Nirala (1896–1961)

The Betrayal

The face yellowed.
The spine curved. The hands joined.
Darkness rose in the eyes.
Centuries passed.
The great sages, saints, and poets arrived.
Each laid down the law.

Some said that one is three,
Others that three is three.
Some felt the pulse, some watched the lotus.
Some revelled, some kissed the fingers.
The people said, 'Blessed are we.'
But the tambourine held out.
The *mridanga* split into the *tabla.*
The *vina* became the *surbahar.*
We now hear the spinet.
The day breaks.
The lips of the four cardinals redden.
Morning's polecats are like night's.
The Age of Betrayal betrays us.

Translated from Hindi by Arvind
Krishna Mehrotra

M. Gopalakrishna Adiga (1918–92)

Do Something, Brother

Do something, brother:
keep doing something, anything;
you mustn't be idle.
Pull out this plant, nip this little leaf,
crush that flower.
There's grass,
run your brand through it,
burn it like Lanka.
Tiny butterflies, parrots, sparrows—
chase them, catch them,
pluck their wings,
pull out their fur and feather.
There, in the garden,
jasmine and the banana's gold
grow for the wild elephant's feet.

All over the walls
virility's master-switches
itch for your fingers;
close your eyes
and pull down twenty of them.
Earth, water, the skies,
they're all your geese with golden eggs:
gouge them out, slash them.
'Do, or die,' they say.
Disasters are the test
for your genius's galloping dance:
something must crash every minute.
Brother, act, act at once, do something.
Thought's weights and measures
are all for the past,
for the undying ghostly treasures of the dead.

There's the forest,
cut it clean to the stump,
slit it for your buntings.
You have the axe, the sickle,
the saw and the knife;
go, harvest all the world
with a flourish of your hand.
But you meet
winter mists, walls of fog,
walls that line the space between face and face,
and the road that sighs and breaks in two
under your eyes,
a couple of mountain-peaks that rear their hoods
and lower upon your head,
or lightning-winks from sirens
that sing in every tree:
do they plunge you into anxieties
and dilemmas of reason?
No, no, this won't do.
You're a simple man, and that's your strength.
Horse-sense and the blinkers
are your forte.

Eat what comes to hand; crush what you touch;
cut the hindering vines.
Mother Earth herself, though tired,
lies open to the skies;
there's still flesh on her bone,
marrow for your hunger.
Come, come, brother,
never forget that you're a man!

Then there's the Well of Life.
Rope the wheel and axle,
pull out all the water.
Reach the last dryness of the rock;
grope, grope with the grappling iron.
'V for Victory,' brother.
Break down the atom,
reach for the ultimate world within.
Find God's own arrow
and aim it straight at the heart
of God's own embryo-world.
Do something, anything,
anything, brother.
Idle men
are burdens on the land.
Do, brother, do something.
Keep doing something all the time
to lighten Mother Earth's loads.
This is right. This is natural.
This is the one thing needful.

Translated from Kannada by A.K. Ramanujan

Mangesh Padgaonkar (*b.* 1929)

Salaam

Salaam,
to everyone, salaam,
to the hand that holds
and brandishes the rod, salaam,
with my left hand on my rear
for fear of the boot,
a right-handed salaam,
to the one who closely watches me, salaam,
to the one who doesn't watch and doesn't care, salaam,
to the one who'd like to buy me out, salaam,
to his unseen boss, who orders him to buy me out, salaam,
salaam, dear friends, to everyone, salaam.

To every eye that glares, salaam,
to the holy, bright vermilion stone, salaam,
to the temples that cost a million to build, salaam,
to the awesome power of the gods in their sanctums, salaam,
to those who draw up testimonials
for gurus, idols, and beliefs, salaam,
to the priest who coaxes offerings
from empty, supplicating hands, salaam,
to the priest of priests who conjures up
a diamond ring from empty air, salaam,
to the star of ill-luck, salaam,
to the star of good fortune, salaam,
to father, who snaps at mother all her life, salaam,
to the boss who snaps at father all his life, salaam,
to the boss's boss, who snaps at the boss, salaam,
salaam, dear ladies and gentlemen,
to everyone of you, salaam.

To every eye that scans the morning papers, salaam,
to the men who report and analyse
the speeches and the news, salaam,
to the tycoons who hire and publish them, salaam,

to the men in office cultivating them, salaam,
to the face that faces microphones and cameras, salaam,
to the mouth that pours its verbiage into them, salaam,
to the millions who wait and watch
and listen and believe, salaam,
to the master hypnotists who practise all their skills on them,
     salaam,
salaam, dear friends, to everyone, salaam.

   To the streetcorner tough, salaam,
to the bootlegger, toiling incessantly, salaam,
to the smuggler of contraband, salaam,
to the scrupulous, efficient customs men
who let him through, salaam,
to the one who operates a chain
of betting shops and gambling dens, salaam,
to the cops on the beat who're fed and fattened by him,
     salaam,
to the tyranny of the autocrat, salaam,
to the tyranny of the people, also, salaam,
to the man who drives the van of power, salaam,
to the luckless wretches, the curs,
who're crushed beneath its wheels, salaam,
to the hand that draws the sword, salaam,
to the hand that ejects a bomb from a plane, salaam,
to the enormous traffickers in weaponry, salaam,
to black-market men, salaam,
to those who announce, at periodic intervals,
that all black-market men shall soon be hanged, salaam,
to doctors, surgeons, homeopaths, salaam,
to their mounting cures and insurmountable bills, salaam,
to those who retail the accessories for the last rites, salaam,
to those who lend their shoulders
to bear the last remains, salaam,
to all who deal and delight in death, salaam,
salaam, dear ladies, dear gentlemen,
to every one of you, salaam.

   To rat-holes, salaam,
to the rats in those rat-holes, salaam,

to the roaches who encroach
on kitchens and cabinets, salaam,
to the lice that breed in beards, salaam,
to the haggard, life-long wife, salaam,
to the half-fed child in the half-shared room in a tenement slum,
    salaam,
to the nameless, faceless throngs in buses and in trains, salaam,
to the pest-infested grain, salaam,
to the secret ownership of factories, salaam,
to the corpulent men who lead the workers' unions, salaam,
to the workers who slave and the workers who strike, salaam,
to the fight-to-the-end for food and cash, salaam,
to every flag of every colour of every kind, salaam,
to the lumps that harden in latrines, salaam,
to every vice-like grip on the throat, salaam,
salaam, my old familiars,
to each of you, respectfully, salaam.

   To this my supremely sacred, etcetera, native land, salaam,
to this my country's marvellous magnificence, salaam,
to all its neolithic heritage, salaam,
to the dung-heap of caste and class, salaam,
to those who draw from this dung their rights and destinies,
    salaam,
to the Vedas and the Upanishads, salaam,
to the lords and scions who preserve
their feudal acres and servile underlings, salaam,
to those elected rightfully, salaam,
to their right to raise and use
enormous campaign-funds, salaam,
to unseen, stone-hard fists, salaam,
to the stone-blind hands that stamp the ballot-papers, salaam,
to all political parties, salaam,
to their thoughtfully chosen symbols of cows and elephants,
    salaam,
to those in their ranks who're paid to silence and rape,
    salaam,
to those who assault the naked and the starved, salaam,
to all the emasculated men who read the news about these,

salaam,
salaam, dear friends, to everyone, salaam.

Call it a country of usurers and quacks,
and they will shout you down;
call it a country run by truants, bribers, sycophants,
and they will rough you up;
call it a mob of touts and auction-clerks and mafia-men,
and they will crack your skull;
make fun of religion and politics, like this,
and they will strip your wife and children:
so, first of all,
to this, my own emasculation, salaam,
then, to every hand that brandishes the rod
and hits, salaam,
and then, as I was taught,
to this supremely sacred, etcetera, mother-land, salaam,
to this great land's redoubtable ancient ways, salaam.

Salaam,
dear ladies and gentlemen,
to every one of you, a reverential salaam.
If I had several arms and hands,
like all our sacred pantheon,
with every one of them I would have salaamed.
Forgive me, mortal as I am,
that I have only two:
the left I reserve for my rear,
and with the right I offer you
a simple, one-handed salaam.

Salaam, dear ladies and gentlemen, to everyone, salaam.

Translated from Marathi by Vinay Dharwadker

Afterword:
Modern Indian Poetry and its Contexts

Vinay Dharwadker

1

Like poems written elsewhere and at other times, modern Indian poems are connected to the larger world in which they exist in numerous, often complicated ways. One of the most common connections consists of the verbal references and representational strategies with which a poem points to, talks about, or even incorporates something in its historical situation or social environment. Another familiar link appears when a poem relates to the world through the life and works of its author, as well as the memories and imaginations of its readers, whom it affects and sometimes changes. A third connection surfaces in the institutions that give a poem its material form, put it into circulation, help it to survive, and thus make it a vital part of its world. Yet one more link takes the form of a poem's embodiment or incarnation in a specific language, its acceptance of a set of codes and conventions, its absorption into a well-defined literary tradition, and so on. Because of this multiplicity of references, relationships, and connections (more of which can be listed), modern Indian poems—like other poems—derive much of their meaningfulness and meaning, their cultural value and imaginative power, from their various contexts.

Reading modern Indian poetry in context, however, can be difficult and confusing, because the contexts often appear simultaneously at local, regional, and national levels, and involve not only the situation of a poem in relation to its author, readers, language, and tradition, but also the relationships between that language and the other Indian languages and their histories and cultures. A contextual discussion of modern Indian poetry is nevertheless essential, since it gives us a historical account of the poetry in the various mother tongues (individually and together), relates the words and qualities of specific poems to specific events, institutions, and practices, explains why certain poems have certain features and not others, reveals how the poetry changes by language and region and yet remains interconnected across the subcontinent, and so on. All this helps us as readers to clear up obscurities, resolve some ambiguities, make comparisons and judgments, discover generalities and patterns, and take up positions, arriving at what we think of as an understanding of modern Indian poetry.

In this essay, I have not tried to provide a comprehensive contextual account of twentieth-century poetry in the fifteen languages represented here. Such an account is simply not possible at present, given the state of literary studies in and relating to contemporary India. Rather, I have provisionally and selectively focused on three broad contexts, which enable us to see how modern Indian poems are connected to each other and to their extremely heterogeneous world. These contexts give us a basic historical, literary, and social framework within which we can situate individual poems and poets as well as specific languages and traditions. Some such framework needs to be established before we can develop a more adequate critical narrative for the immensely crowded, complex, and fascinating story of nineteenth- and twentieth-century Indian poetry as a whole.

2

One of the principal historical contexts of modern Indian poetry is the variety of movements, counter-movements, schools, factions, and styles that have shaped it during the past one hundred years or so. Throughout the twentieth century, schools and movements have appeared all over the country in significant numbers and with great regularity. Some of them have been national in scope, bringing together most of the languages, while others have been local or regional in character, being confined to one or two languages and communities. Some have lasted for a quarter of a century or more, and have involved more than one generation of writers. Others, however, have survived less than a decade, and have been centred around small (but influential) coteries of friends. Most of the successful poetic movements have also produced large quantities of other work—ranging from manifestos, critical essays, and conference proceedings to famous magazines and popular anthologies—which follow different paths of innovation and change. The resulting variety has complicated the course of Indian poetry since the end of the nineteenth century, often creating one set of patterns at the national level and another at the local and regional levels, and generating unexpected continuities and discontinuities among the languages.

In the first half of the twentieth century, for example, a series of successive, overlapping, and interacting movements appeared at the national level, which prepared the ground for the mixture of schools and styles we find in contemporary India. The earliest of these emerged between about 1900 and 1930, when the various languages collectively went through a phase of intensely nationalist writing. This movement, which had its origins in the nineteenth century, included hundreds of popular poets who wrote (or tried to write) rousing poems about Mother India, her glorious, heroic, and ancient past, her present courage in the face of British imperialism, and her determination to win her political and cultural freedom in the near future. It also included dozens of more serious poets, most of whom played prominent roles in the freedom movement, both locally and nationally. Among them were figures like Rabindranath Tagore (Bengali) and Aurobindo Ghose (English), whose work is still read widely, as well as poets like Shridhar Pathak, Maithilisharan Gupta, and Makhanlal Chaturvedi (Hindi), whose work is now read by smaller regional audiences and mainly—one hopes—for its historical interest. During the nationalist movement, Indian poetry as a whole seemed to be at one with its social and political circumstances, and the poets seemed to be equally at one with their audiences. In subsequent movements, these identifications were to give way to 'alienation' between poems and their immediate situations and between poets and their publics.

Between the two World Wars, and especially between about 1920 and 1935, the Indian languages passed through a new nation-wide phase of 'Romantic' writing (an earlier, longer one had appeared in the nineteenth century), which overlapped with the nationalist movement. In this phase a large number of poets attempted to redo, at least in part, what the Romantics in England had done more than a century earlier. The models for these poets included the better-known works of William Words-worth, John Keats, and Percy Bysshe Shelley, the minor lyrics of Lord Byron, and the poems of lesser figures like Thomas Hood (as well as the writings of Sir Walter Scott, Lord Alfred Tennyson, and Henry Wadsworth Longfellow). This type of displaced and modified Romanticism appeared, for example, in Assamese, in the work of Lakshminath Bezbarua, Raghunath Raichoudhary, and Jatindranath Duara; in Telugu, in the Bhavakavitvam school of poetry led by Rayaprolu Subbarao and Devulapalli Krishna Sastri; and in Marathi, in the poetry of Balkavi and that of Madhav Julian and the poets of the Ravi Kiran Mandal. By and large, the twentieth-century Indian Romantic movement empha-sized the primacy of the unique human individual and his or her unified sensibility, concentrating on 'intense personal ex-perience', emotional spontaneity, lyricism, and sincerity to produce a body of writing that dealt mainly with nature, love, desire, melancholy, childhood, simplicity, nostalgia, and fine feelings. These private, often idiosyncratic explorations general-ly contrasted sharply with the public rhetoric of nationalist poetry, and created a distance between the poet and his or her audience and the text and its contexts. But they contributed nonetheless to the definition of a distinctive modern Indian self and even an alternative national identity, in which a poet intro-spectively and 'privately' (rather than 'publicly') became the site where one or more Indian literary traditions asserted or manifested themselves.

Two new, frequently intersecting and simultaneous national movements appeared in the 1930s to complicate the dialectic of nationalism and romanticism. One was the movement launched effectively by the national conference of the Progres-sive Writers' Association at Lucknow in 1936 (with a presidential address by Munshi Premchand, the foremost fiction writer in modern Hindi). The Progressive movement, some of whose early proponents continued to write until the 1980s, emphasized the significance of Marxist thought and socialist and communist ideals for the various Indian literatures, especially Urdu, Hindi, Bengali, Gujarati, Marathi, English, Telugu, Kannada, and Malayalam. It included, deeply influenced, or indirectly affected—sometimes only much later in time—a number of the poets represented in these pages: among them, Nirala, G.M. Muktibodh, Shamsher Bahadur Singh, Raghuvir Sahay, Sarveshwar Dayal Saxena, Kedarnath Singh, and Dhoomil (all Hindi); B.S. Mardhekar, Vinda Karandikar, Namdeo Dhasal, and Narayan Surve (all Marathi); Sri Sri (Telugu), Ali Sardar Jafri (Urdu), Adil Jussawalla (English), and Bishnu De and Subhash Mukhopadhyay (Bengali). Many of the Progressive writers criticized and rejected the patriotism and romanticism of their predecessors, and attempted to paint a bleak, often starkly violent, even 'anti-nationalistic' portrait of Indian society, choosing invective, satire, and irony over epic seriousness and lyricism. Of the poems included here, Nirala's 'The Betrayal', Muktibodh's 'The Void', Dhoomil's 'The City, Evening, and an Old Man: Me', Mukhopadhyay's 'The Task', Jafri's 'Morsel', Sri Sri's 'Some People Laugh, Some People Cry', and Jussawalla's 'Sea Breeze, Bombay' are examples of work influenced by the Progressive movement at various points between about 1940 and 1975.

The other nation-wide movement that started in the 1930s —and continued to affect writers and readers until the end of the 1970s—was the Indian counterpart of Anglo-American modernism, in which poets in practically every language broke away from traditional (often highly Sanskritized) metres, stanza patterns, styles, materials, and themes to invent 'free verse' poetry. In exploring new forms of writing, these poets often took up distinctively high modernist positions (for example, in Marathi, B.S. Mardhekar in the 1940s), or combined them with existentialist perspectives in the Indian context (Vinda Karandikar in the 1950s), or with avant garde, especially surrealist, viewpoints (Dilip Chitre and Arun Kolatkar in the 1960s). Using a range of this sort, they concentrated on such themes as the disintegration of traditional communities and familiar cultural institutions, the alienation of the individual in urban society, the dissociation of thought and feeling, the disasters of modernization, the ironies of daily existence, and the anguish of un-resolved doubts and anxieties. Among the numerous poets who contributed significantly to this movement in their mother tongues were writers like Jibanananda Das and Buddhadeva Bose (Bengali), Gopalakrishna Adiga and K.S. Narasimhaswami (Kannada), Umashankar Joshi (Gujarati), Nissim Ezekiel (English), B.S. Mardhekar, P.S. Rege, and Vinda Karandikar (Marathi), and Nirala, Agyeya, and G.M. Muktibodh (Hindi). Das's 'In Camp', Adiga's 'Do Something, Brother', Narasimha-swami's 'Consolation to Empty Pitchers', Mardhekar's 'The Forest of Yellow Bamboo Trees', Karandikar's 'The Knot', and Shrikant Verma's 'The Pleasure Dome' are good instances of early and late Indian experiments in poetry of the modernist kind. As these examples should suggest, the continuities and discontinuities which mark the relationships among the major national literary movements of the first half of the twentieth century frame many of the schools and styles of poetry repre-sented in this anthology.

While movements of the kind described above have emerged steadily at the national level through much of the twentieth century, the literary culture of each language has also developed more local and regional schools, factions, and styles. During the past eight or nine decades, Hindi poetry, for in-stance, has passed through several successive and concurrent movements, some unique to it and several linked directly to the nation-wide movements. This makes the history of Hindi poetry in the twentieth century distinct from that of twentieth-century Indian poetry as a whole, while at the same time linking the two histories in a number of ways.

In the 1910s and 1920s, for example, many Hindi poets banded together under the label of *adarshavad* or 'idealism', a school of high-minded poetry concerned with pure moral and cultural ideals, led by poets like Maithilisharan Gupta and Ram-naresh Tripathi. This movement started as a regional one in the Hindi-speaking area, but soon became central to the larger movement of political and cultural nationalism contemporan-eous with it. *Adarshavad*, in fact, served as a principal instrument for the ascendency of the Hindi-speaking population of north India in national cultural politics during the early years of the inter-war period. However, almost immediately after World War I, Jayashankar Prasad, Nirala, Sumitranandan Pant, and Mahadevi Verma launched *chhayavad*, literally 'shadow-ism' (a name given by its detractors) which was influenced by the English Romantics as well as Tagore, especially the latter's explorations of pre-modern Indian religious and philosophical thought, spiritualism, and mysticism. This movement rejected the poetics and politics of *adarshavad* and produced, among other notable things, a poetry of intimate moods and obscure desires, a lyrical nature poetry, an other-worldly poetry of love and longing for the divine, and a confessional poetry of despair and anguish. It resembled the Romantic movements of the time in other parts of the country, but the Hindi poets developed striking personal styles and public presences (especially Nirala and Mahadevi), which made them and their work rather unusual on the national scene.

Just before World War II, Kedarnath Agrawal, Ramvilas Sharma, Trilochan Shastri, Shamsher Bahadur Singh, and a number of other writers inaugurated *pragativad* or 'progressivism' in Hindi, and around the same time poets like Agyeya, Girijakumar Mathur, and Prabhakar Machwe began practising *prayogavad*, or 'experimentalism'. These two schools of Hindi poetry corresponded rather closely with the progressive and modernist movements at the national level. However, in the 1950s, the twin streams of 'progressivism' and 'experimentalism' merged into the crowded movement in Hindi called *nai kavita*, or 'the new poetry', which brought together Shamsher, Agyeya, and G.M. Muktibodh (among others) in their later phases, as well as Kunwar Narain, Kedarnath Singh, Shrikant Verma, Raghuvir Sahay, and Sarveshwar Dayal Saxena in their early phases. *Nai kavita* explicitly rejected the poetics of *chhayavad* and produced a large mixture of experimental, social, and political poetry that drew a great deal of national attention for its unusual range and quality. In effect (and especially in retrospect), the *nai kavita* movement in Hindi was very different from the corresponding 'new poetry' movements of the 1950s in, say, Kannada and Marathi.

After about 1965, *nai kavita* was partially displaced by several schools or movements of anti-poetry and protest poetry, variously labelled *akavita* ('non-poetry'), *pratirodh ki kavita* ('the poetry of opposition'), and so on. Around 1970, these schools were sidelined in turn by the new, politically radical work of poets like Saxena (in his later phase) and Dhoomil, which had the effect of turning Hindi poetry in a direction different from that of the poetry of the time in, say, Gujarati, Oriya, or Tamil. In the 1980s, this flow was disrupted and re-directed especially by the appearance of a new generation of women poets, such as Gagan Gill, Archana Varma, and Jyotsna Milan, a number of whom write from overtly feminist viewpoints. Following these shifts and changes, *samkaleen kavita* or 'contemporary poetry' in Hindi is now a wide assortment of old and new schools and styles, many of them carried over with mutations from the last four or five decades.

Of the poems included in this anthology, Sumitranandan Pant's 'Almora Spring' is a representative descriptive nature poem in the *chhayavad* mode, while Shamsher Bahadur Singh's 'On the Slope of This Hill' is a fairly typical early Progressive poem in Hindi. In contrast, Agyeya's 'Hiroshima' is an example of a cosmopolitan, 'humanistic' *nai kavita* poem; Saxena's 'The Black Panther' is an instance of political symbolism and con-densed/allegory from the 1970s; whereas Kedarnath Singh's 'On Reading a Love Poem' and Gagan Gill's 'The Girl's Desire Moves Among Her Bangles' are examples of *samkaleen kavita* from the early and late 1980s, respectively. To grasp the divergences be-tween, say, Hindi and Gujarati poetry with regard to their respec-tive progressive, experimental, and 'new poetry' phases, one would have to compare the poems by Pant, Shamsher, and Agyeya mentioned above, as well as the poems by Dhoomil and Sarveshwar Dayal Saxena in this volume, with the 'landscape' poems in Gujarati by Umashankar Joshi, Ghulam Mohammed Sheikh, Ravji Patel, and Sitanshu Yashashchandra. Similarly, to understand the historical and qualitative differences between Hindi or Gujarati poetry on the one hand, and Kannada poetry on the other, one would have to place the above-mentioned poems beside the poems about landscapes and places by Gopala-krishna Adiga, Chandrashekhar Kambar, and K.S. Narasimha-swami represented here.

As a synoptic account of this sort suggests, factions, schools, movements, and counter-movements constitute the historical mechanics of poetic change in the Indian situation, at the local as well as regional and national levels. Movements often give poets their basic world-views and literary orientations, demarcate their politics, suggest their subjects and themes, and shape their styles, strategies, techniques, and images. They show us how to differentiate one kind of poetry from another, assess intentions and attitudes, and interpret particular poetic qualities and effects. More importantly, they begin to explain the great diversity of writing we find in each language and across languages at any given moment, as well as the common factors which connect languages and traditions to each other over time.

3

A second major context of nineteenth- and twentieth-century Indian poetry is the variety of Indian and foreign literatures surrounding it. In the web of intertextual relationships spreading outwards from this poetry, 'foreign influences' have played a crucial role in the emergence of Indian modernity. The same is true of the older literatures of the subcontinent, which constitute the 'domestic sources' that Indian poets have constantly plundered in their quest for novelty, modernity, and meaning. Reading modern Indian poems in the context of various literatures and literary relationships helps us to explain phenomena that we cannot explain easily by analysing the history of poetic movements.

Indian sources and foreign influences play different kinds of roles, with each also serving several distinct purposes. Some foreign influences work at the level where an entire Western literature deeply affects one or more modern Indian literatures. English literature is an obvious case in point, because it has pervasively influenced all the Indian language traditions since the nineteenth century. Other Western literatures also enter the picture, but they work differently and differentially. For instance, poets from Bengal, whether they write in Bengali or English or both, have had a more or less unique, obsessive relationship with the French language and its literature for almost a hundred and fifty years now. 'The French Connection' first appeared in Bengal around the third quarter of the nineteenth century, in the work and careers of poets like Michael Madhusudan Dutt (Bengali and English) and Toru Dutt (English). It then resurfaced strongly just before and soon after the middle of the twentieth century in the generations represented by, say, Buddhadeva Bose and Nabaneeta Dev Sen (both bilingual in Bengali and English), who have extensively worked out rather agnostic connections with Baudelaire, Mallarmé, Rimbaud, and Valéry. Some of the distinctive qualities of modern Bengali poetry—for instance, its immersion in metropolitan culture, its love-hate relationship with modernity, its simultaneous provincialism and cosmopolitanism, its zeal for revolutions—carry strong traces of French influence. The Bengali situation is intriguing because exact parallels in the other Indian languages appear only piecemeal in the work of individual poets, as when we find a strong interest in the French symbolists and twentieth-century avant garde poets in, say, Arun Kolatkar and Dilip Chitre (both bilingual in Marathi and English).

The anomaly of the situation of French literature in India is heightened by its contrast with two other prominent foreign literatures. Spanish poetry from Latin America, particularly the work of Pablo Neruda (probably the single most influential poet in the world in recent times), has generated a much more evenly spread interest among poets in different Indian languages, whether Bengali and Hindi, or Gujarati, Oriya, and Malayalam. Similarly, American Beat poetry of the 1950s and 1960s has also had a widespread effect, chiefly through the influence of Allen Ginsberg, drawing strong (favourable) responses from all over the subcontinent. Neither of these bodies of writing, however, has yet affected Indian poetry as deeply as English Romantic, Victorian, and high modernist writing has, or for a comparable length of time.

In the modern Indian situation, foreign influences work not only at the level of whole literatures and movements, but also at the level of specific genres, and at that of isolated connections between individual authors. In the case of genres, between the first quarter of the nineteenth century and the third quarter of the twentieth, for example, the English and European sonnet has predictably seduced many strong and weak poets in languages like Bengali, Marathi, English, and Urdu; while in recent decades the Japanese haiku has sparked off experiments in, say, Kannada. It is worth observing that the mechanics of imitation, derivation, and transfer also appear in the case of modern Indian prose, where, for instance, the nineteenth-century Russian short story—Chekhov, Turgenev, Dostoevsky, Tolstoi—remained an obvious primary model for Indian writers for more than half a century.

In contrast, in the case of particular influences on individual writers, we find a much wider range of obsessions and affiliations, some of them quite startling: for example, Vinda Karandikar's interest in Gerard Manley Hopkins, B.S. Mardhekar's in T.S. Eliot, Mangesh Padgaonkar's in W.H. Auden, B.C. Ramachandra Sharma's in W.B. Yeats, and Gurunath Dhuri's in Stephen Spender (all British or Anglo-Irish); Subramania Bharati's in Walt Whitman and Dilip Chitre's in Hart Crane (both American); Sitanshu Yashashchandra's in Nicanor Parra (Chilean) and G.M. Muktibodh's in Cesare Pavese (Italian); as well as, say, Shrikant Verma's in Aimé Césaire (French Caribbean), Octavio Paz (Mexican), and Andrei Voznesensky (Russian), and Kedarnath Singh's in hans magnus enzensberger (German) and Vasko Popa (Serbo-Croatian). Yashashchandra's 'Drought' and Singh's 'On Reading a Love Poem' obviously owe some of their techniques, concerns, and effects to Latin American and European models, respectively. But they are far from derivative poems—in fact, they have so thoroughly absorbed and transmuted their 'foreign influences' that they themselves have become landmarks of innovation and originality.

If the context of foreign literatures helps us to unravel lines of influence in the network of modernity, the context of Indian literatures allows us to separate the varieties of revival, retrieval, reworking, and renovation that revitalize the Indian poetic imagination on its home ground. Although all modern poets 'reject' the past in order to become 'modern', they often end up using the past imaginatively and constructively in a multitude of ways: many modern writers are, quite paradoxically, traditionalists and classicists. We find modern Indian poets replicating this paradox from a variety of poetic, political, and philosophical positions. Thus, in the third quarter of the nineteenth century, for instance, Michael Madhusudan Dutt (Bengali) inverted and retold a part of the *Ramayana* story in his *Meghanadbadh*, which became a classic of modern Bengali and Indian poetry; while in the second quarter of the twentieth century, Jayashankar Prasad (Hindi) incorporated Sanskrit myth, prosody, poetics, and philosophy with extensions rather than inversions in his lyric and epic poems, which struck a very contemporary note in their time.

In a similar vein, since the turn of the century numerous poets have drawn extensively on the forms, devices, voices, and motifs of the *bhakti* poetry produced in the Dravidian and Indo-Aryan languages during the past one thousand years or more. Mahadevi Varma (Hindi) and Indira Sant (Marathi), for example, have revitalized Mirabai's sixteenth-century Rajasthani poetry of love, separation, and union with a divine lover (*viraha bhakti*), combining it with nineteenth-century English Romanticism; B.S. Mardhekar and Vinda Karandikar have turned to the examples of Jnaneshwar (thirteenth century) and Tukaram (seventeenth century) in Marathi; Arun Kolatkar has fused Jnaneshwar and Tukaram, among others, with Rimbaud, the dadaists, the surrealists, and the Beat poets; and Nagarjuna (Hindi) has attempted a large-scale elaboration of the north Indian Kabir tradition (fifteenth century). Correspondingly, in the past two or three decades, Nissim Ezekiel (English) has used classical Sanskrit models to produce delightful experimental poster poems; Arvind Krishna Mehrotra (English) has exploited second-century Prakrit originals to write witty, epigrammatic poems; Bishnu De (Bengali) has incorporated oral Santhal tribal songs into written forms in a standardized literary language; while Ravji Patel (Gujarati) has reworked folk formulas and oral structures into surreal contemporary lyrics. Significantly enough, Rabindranath Tagore (Bengali) and Subramania Bharati (Tamil) perfected many of these strategies on a large scale around the beginning of this century: they drew boldly on Vedic hymns, Upanishadic dialogues, Vedantic concepts, and *bhakti* poems; on Baul songs in Bengali, religious-erotic poetry in Maithili, or proverbs and riddles in Tamil; and on grandmothers' tales, nursery rhymes, lullabies, and even abecedariums. Bharati's 'Wind, 9', De's 'Santhal Poems, 1', and

Ravji Patel's 'Whirlwind', as well as two magnificent longer pieces—Chandrashekhar Kambar's 'A Pond Named Ganga' and G. Shankara Kurup's 'The Master Carpenter'—are among the numerous poems in this book which demonstrate how Indian literary sources function as a major context for modern Indian poetry.

If modern Indian poetry draws intertextually on many different literatures and is a product of many different movements and schools of poetry, then it is bound to be extremely varied. Not surprisingly, in the pile of hundreds of thousands of modern Indian poems, we find pieces of every shade and colour, every shape and size. In terms of religious material and position, for example, we find that Tagore's 'Flute-music' (Bengali) carves out a specifically Vaishnava space for itself, while Jayashankar Prasad's *Kamayani* (Hindi) chooses a Shaiva orientation within a broadly Hindu framework; Khalil-ur-Rahman Azmi's 'I and "I"' (Urdu) works specifically with Islam and Muslim identity, while Paresh Chandra Raut's 'Snake' (Oriya) invokes Christian myth and Biblical imagery; Keki Daruwalla's 'A Parsi Hell' (English) confronts a Parsi heritage, whereas Daya Pawar's 'The Buddha' (Marathi) revives Buddhist stories and history; and in contrast to all these, Nissim Ezekiel's 'Latter-Day Psalms' (English) combines a Bene-Israel Jewish background with a tragic humanistic vision.

Similarly, in terms of poetic form, we encounter the full range of possibilities even within the limited scope of this book. We find the short imagistic poem in Nirmalprabha Bardoloi (Assamese) and Anuradha Mahapatra (Bengali); the modern satiric poem in quatrains in B.C. Ramachandra Sharma (Kannada) and B.S. Mardhekar (Marathi); the dramatic lyric in Sunanda Tripathy (Oriya); the relatively abstract contemplative poem in Jayanta Mahapatra (English) and the sombre meditative poem in Rajani Parulekar (Marathi); the long poetic sequence in Subramania Bharati (Tamil) and Nissim Ezekiel (English) and the short sequence in K.V. Tirumalesh (Kannada); the symbolist long poem in Jibanananda Das (Bengali); the surreal love poem in Aziz Qaisi (Urdu); the folk-didactic 'kitchen poem' in Bahinabai Chaudhari (Marathi); the stock feminist poem in A. Jayaprabha (Telugu) and Popati Hira-

nandani (Sindhi); the descriptive and evocative place poem in
Ghulam Mohammed Sheikh (Gujarati); the densely allusive cul-
tural and ecological satire in Gopalakrishna Adiga (Kannada);
and the dark confessional poem in Kamala Das (English). The
range of thematic and formal choices and affiliations generated
by such convergences of linguistic, literary, and cultural contexts
is probably best represented by (the late) A.K. Ramanujan's
poetry, equally distinguished in both English and Kannada,
which brings together Cassandra and the *Mundaka Upanishad*,
the Tamil *cankam* poets and the Kannada *bhakti* poets, Pascal
and Yeats, *King Lear* and *Four Quartets*, pointillism and Zen, César
Vallejo and René Char, the imagistic lyric and the satiric prose
poem, as well as the modernist meditation and the postmodern-
ist collage, crossing numerous poetic and historical boundaries
in the process. This great variety of voices and echoes, shapes
and forms—which should be evident in every section of the
anthology—highlights the intertexture of modern Indian poetry
with a wide range of sources, influences, conventions, and litera-
tures, that are variously local and regional, folk and canonical,
national and international.

4

A third crucial context of modern Indian poetry is its varied
social world, which shapes the lives of the poets, their education
and literary training, their relationships with their medium and
their audiences, their understanding of the conventions and
functions of authorship, as well as their identities in a rapidly
changing literary culture. The heterogeneity of the Indian social
world permeates many different literary institutions, takes the
form of synchronic variations as well as historical transforma-
tions, and surfaces at several distinct levels of analysis.

For example, the heterogeneity is evident in the fact that
all modern Indian writers do not come from the same social
class. It is true that the majority of modern Indian writers consists
of middle-class men and women, but the so-called middle-class
in India is itself a spectrum of different positions, varying by
language, region, religion, caste, occupation, income, educa-
tion, degree of urbanization, and so on (with its lower segments

living below the line that defines 'poverty' in Europe and America). But even though this makes it possible to claim that the Indian literatures by and large are a middle-class phenomenon, it is important to remember that some Indian writers come from upper-class backgrounds (for example, Rabindranath Tagore and Sudhindranath Dutta earlier, and Arun Joshi, Salman Rushdie, and Bharati Mukherjee now), while others, in increasing numbers in recent decades, come from low-income families in large cities and small towns (for instance, G.M. Muktibodh), impoverished village communities in the countryside (Bahinabai Chaudhari, Anuradha Mahapatra), and even the bottomless bottom of the caste hierarchy (Daya Pawar, Namdeo Dhasal, Hira Bansode, Jyoti Lanjewar, Narayan Surve).

In fact, when we survey the modern Indian literatures systematically, they turn out to constitute an essentially mixed institution that draws writers as well as readers and audiences from many different parts of the Indian social world. Thus, among the best-known recent poets in the major languages—such as those represented here—we find businessmen, politicians, commercial artists, economists, doctors, physicists, school-teachers, teachers of education, professors of language and literature (often teaching literatures other than their own), clerks, local administrators, national-level bureaucrats, social workers, journalists, editors, song-writers and screen-play writers in the film industry, advertising executives, philosophers, art-critics, housewives, factory-workers, former street-dwellers and wage-labourers, and full-time writers. This makes the twentieth-century Indian poetic world heterogeneous, unpredictable, and exciting when compared to the sedate or colourless literary worlds we sometimes find elsewhere.

Nor do all modern Indian poets study literature formally beyond the high-school level: their education in college ranges from Sanskrit and the fine arts, to law, the natural sciences, and engineering. Most of them acquire or develop their literary tastes outside the institutional classroom, most often in local networks of writers, translators, critics, intellectuals, and 'activists' of various shades and colours who meet in coffee-houses and tea-stalls, private homes and campus common-rooms, or even at cinema theatres, movie clubs, libraries, and art-galleries. The liveliest and most influential modern Indian writing still comes out of these 'autonomous associations' characteristic of a 'civil society' in which writers write chiefly in order to exercise their common citizenship, both politically and apolitically, as fully as possible.

The principal medium in which modern Indian poets exercise their citizenship is, of course, the medium of print. Their work appears constantly in mass-media weeklies and monthlies, small literary magazines, institutional journals, edited anthologies, individual books, and posthumous editions of collected works. In some cases, a language may have more than a dozen periodicals that publish poetry regularly (e.g., English, Bengali, Hindi); in others, there may be less than a handful (e.g., Assamese, Dogri). The languages with the ten or twelve largest populations of native speakers have large (sometimes very large) regional publishing industries, and in each of them there are several publishers who concentrate on contemporary literature. In a language like Bengali, Hindi, or Marathi, at least a couple of hundred poets publish their work in any given year; most of them appear in magazines, but a substantial number of them also publish books, some privately, some with small presses, and others with well-known publishing houses. An established poet may sell between 2,000 and 5,000 copies of a book of poems over five years or so; a good anthology of contemporary poetry may sell out two or three such editions in a single decade. The modern classics and literary bestsellers in each language— Tagore in Bengali, Ghalib in Urdu, Deokinandan Khatri and Premchand in Hindi prose—run into forty or fifty large printings in the course of a century.

Contemporary Indian poets and their audiences, however, do not communicate only through the abstract medium of print. They come face to face at poetry readings organized by colleges, literary societies, libraries, and private cultural centres and state academies, as well as by political groups and political parties. They congregate at local, state, and national writers' conferences and at international cultural festivals. Besides, the poets now travel abroad on exchange programmes between national governments, as participants in reading circuits set up by Indian embassies and Indian immigrants' associations and networks, and at the invitation of international book-fair and cultural-festival committees. They spend time in the Soviet Union and Bulgaria on state-sponsored junkets (now a thing of the past), in the United States at private universities and liberal arts colleges, in Australia and Great Britain 'at the behest' of Arts Councils. They meet readers and listeners in Frankfurt, Toronto, Washington, and Singapore.

The consequences of this new mobility can be quite ironic. Thus, some of the cosmopolitan poets find themselves staying at home, reading García Márquez, Borges, Fanon, Spivak, Said, Pynchon, Larkin, Heaney, Yevtushenko, Achebe, Soyinka, Faiz, themselves, and each other. At the same time, some of the proponents of provincialism and Indianness end up spending time in Queens and at Disney World, visiting newly immigrant sons and sons-in-law, brothers and life-long friends, and photographing Mickey Mouse and watching American music videos. The readers and listeners they reach are equally varied and scattered: politically partisan 'mass audiences' in Belgaum and Aurangabad, small groups of writers and academics at the local Max Müller Bhavan or the Alliance Française, the fashionable set at the India International Centre, and coteries of expatriate Indians and South Asia specialists in London and Chicago.

The picture of the modern Indian poets' varied world is complicated by the fact that many of them have been and are writers and intellectuals or artists in the larger sense. Besides poems, they publish short stories, novellas, and novels, plays and literary criticism, essays on social issues and travel accounts. Amrita Pritam, for example, is not only the best-known contemporary woman poet in Punjabi, but also the most important modern writer in the language in general, with more than seventy collections of poems and short stories, novels, autobiographical accounts, and other kinds of works to her credit. At another level of accomplishment, a younger writer like Jagannath Prasad Das has published volumes of poetry in Oriya and English, plays in Oriya that have been translated into Hindi, English, Punjabi, and Bengali, as well as collections of short stories in Oriya, and has edited anthologies of contemporary Oriya fiction and poetry in English translation. At a more general cultural level, painter-poets like Ghulam Mohammed Sheikh and Gieve Patel are as central to the history of modern Gujarati poetry and Indian English poetry, respectively, as they are to the history of twentieth-century Indian art, art criticism, and aesthetics. At an equally complex level of integration, A.K. Ramanujan combined his career as a bilingual writer of poetry and fiction in English and Kannada with his simultaneous career as a translator. He translated contemporary English materials into Kannada as well as ancient and modern Tamil and Kannada literatures into English, and collaborated with others to translate specific Telugu, Malayalam, and even Sanskrit works into English. As a scholar, theorist, and interpreter of various Indian literatures and cultures, his career was equally diverse.

This variety of artistic achievement is not just a contemporary phenomenon. To mention only two examples, around the middle of this century B.S. Mardhekar invented an influential kind of modern poetry in Marathi, and also wrote experimental novels and plays, as well as the most widely discussed book of literary theory and aesthetics in the language. During the same period, G.M. Muktibodh wrote poetry, short stories and novellas, and a substantial quantity of literary and cultural criticism in an equally innovative mode in Hindi, leaving behind posthumously collected works that now fill eight thick volumes. Historically, the ideal of versatility goes back even further. Between the last two decades of the nineteenth century and the first four decades of the twentieth, Rabindranath Tagore created the most wideranging mixture of this kind, effectively defining the paradigm for future generations: he was a poet, short story writer, novelist, and dramatist, as well as an essayist, critic, autobiographer, travel writer, correspondent, and translator, winning the Nobel Prize for literature in 1913; at the same time, he was also a major lyricist and composer of music, a marvellous painter in his old age, a religious thinker, a nationalist, an anti-nationalist, a national hero, an orator, a public father-figure, a teacher, a theorist of education, and the founder of a major university in Bengal. Given this sort of range, a systematic account of the social contexts of modern Indian poetry is likely to turn rapidly into a full-scale social and cultural history of nineteenth- and twentieth-century India.

5

The heterogeneity of the social world of modern Indian poetry, however, does not end there. In the post-colonial decades, that world has undergone a new series of far-reaching transformations. For one, during the past thirty years it has been altered increasingly and with great effect by the emergence of women poets in the various languages. Until the end of the British Raj, and even in the first decade after Independence, there were few prominent women poets in the country: in the second half of the nineteenth century, for instance, there was Toru Dutt (English); between the two World Wars there were a handful of figures like Sarojini Naidu (English), and Mahadevi Varma and Subhadra Kumari Chauhan (Hindi); and in the final years of colonial rule there were a few younger women like Indira Sant (Marathi) and Balamani Amma (Malayalam). Since the late 1950s, however, the number of women poets in print has risen sharply. This shift is part of the larger, more dramatic trajectory of change Indian women have been creating for themselves in the domestic and public spheres, especially in the domains of literacy, education, journalism, scholarship, the arts, the entertainment industry, politics, and the various modern professions. Between the 1950s and 1970s, we therefore find women poets like Amrita Pritam (Punjabi), Kamala Das (English), and Nabaneeta Dev Sen (Bengali) working concurrently with fiction writers like Qurratulain Hyder (Urdu), Anita Desai and Kamala Markandeya (both English), and Mahashweta Devi (Bengali), scholars like Irawati Karve (Marathi), Romila Thapar and Meenakshi Mukherjee (both English), translators like Lila Ray (Bengali and English), and editors like Madhu Kishwar (English and Hindi) to bring into existence a large, well-defined emergent community of women intellectuals, and a formidable body of women's post-colonial writing in the various languages. In the 1980s there has been virtually an explosion of women's poetry in India, with dozens of new names and voices in English, Marathi, Hindi, Bengali, Oriya, Malayalam, Telugu, and Kannada.

The situation of woman poets in Indian English, in fact, may be a good measure of the change as a whole. In the 1960s the foreground was occupied by relatively isolated figures like Monika Verma and Kamala Das. In the 1970s Gauri Deshpande, Malathi Rao, Anna Sujatha Modayil, Lakshmi Kannan, Mamta Kalia, and Sunita Jain, as well as Eunice de Souza, Melanie Silgardo, Priya Karunakar, Debjani Chatterjee, Nasima Aziz, and Meena Alexander entered the picture, giving it the look of a community of women poets. In the 1980s and early 1990s, Imtiaz Dharker, Tilottama Rajan, Charmayne D'Souza, Shanta Acharya, Menka Shivdasani, and Sujata Bhatt, among others, filled the frame, joining (whether they wanted to or not) the poets who had survived from the previous decades, and giving that community an impressive new profile. Together with their counterparts in the other languages, these women writers have effectively displaced Indian writing from its 'traditional male-dominated centres'.

During the post-colonial decades, the Indian literary world has also been altered by powerful new writers (both men and women) from formerly suppressed or marginal social groups and communities. In the 1960s, and especially in the 1970s, poets from lower-class and lower-caste backgrounds began aggressively and systematically challenging the canons of middle-class and upper-caste literary establishments in languages like Telugu, Kannada, Tamil, and Malayalam, as well as Bengali, Marathi, and Hindi. Many of these 'subaltern' writers came from small towns and communities quite far from the metropolitan centres of Bombay and Calcutta, Delhi and Madras, Lucknow and Hyderabad, writing protest poetry and participating in broader cultural movements in places like Ajmer, Aurangabad, Belgaum, Bhubaneshwar, Ernakulam, Meerut, Nagpur, and Patna. Among the poetic movements that emerged from this wider phenomenon were the Digambara ('naked poetry') movement in Andhra Pradesh, the short-lived Hungry Generation movement in Bengal and the more wide-spread Marxist-Leninist (Naxalite) movement of revolutionary writing in different parts of the country. The best-known movement of this kind, of course, turned out to be the Dalit movement, which began in Maharashtra in the 1950s under the leadership of Dr B.R. Ambedkar, and spread subsequently to neighbouring states like Karnataka as well as to such distant ones as Punjab. The

Maharashtrian Dalits are former untouchables from castes like the Mahars, the Mangs, and the Chamars, who have converted to Buddhism in a collective revolt against the institutions and power structures of Hinduism, and have frequently used poetry, fiction, autobiography, and essays as one of their primary means of political action.

Taken together, the 'subaltern' poets cover a wide range of literary and social positions outside the urban middle class and its institutions. Anuradha Mahapatra, for example, comes from a rural background in Bengal, and is the first person in her family to receive higher education. Bahinabai Chaudhari, who stands on the outermost fringes of modern Indian poetry as a written literature, was an illiterate housewife in a Maharashtrian village who composed and transmitted her poetry orally in the second quarter of this century (her work has come down to us through her son, himself a poet, who wrote down her songs in the last years of her life and published them posthumously). In contrast, Narayan Surve was orphaned at (or soon after) birth, and grew up as a homeless urchin in the streets of Bombay; he survived on charity, wage labour, and odd jobs in the market-place, and taught himself to read and write after reaching maturity. Among the Dalit poets (only Daya Pawar, Namdeo Dhasal, Hirabai Bansode, and Jyoti Lanjewar are included here), Dhasal grew up in the slums of Bombay and became a leader and ideologue of the Dalit Panthers (modelled on the Black Panthers in the United States) before he was twenty-five years old.

As a heterogeneous group of writers from formerly marginal communities, these poets force us to question our most common and far-reaching assumptions about the modern Indian literatures, their social constitution and functions, their canons, aesthetics, and establishments, and their implication in the institutions of power. Converging unexpectedly in the 1970s and 1980s, the women poets and the 'subaltern' poets have broadened and changed the social world of contemporary poetry to an extent we still cannot assess or foresee.

6

The social, literary, and historical contexts discussed in this essay are only selective examples from a broader, more complex range of phenomena that have shaped and reshaped the Indian literatures at the local, regional, and national levels in the course of the nineteenth and twentieth centuries. In the final analysis, however, these contexts do not stand outside the process they are supposed to frame. That large-scale process—which creates new links and breaks among the various Indian languages and poetic traditions, and somehow brings them together and keeps them apart at the same time—seems to absorb texts and contexts into a single undifferentiated continuum, transforming everything simultaneously. It is a process of change that begins and ends over and over again, and as we approach the end of the twentieth century, it appears to have entered a fresh cycle.

In the 1980s a new generation of writers appeared in print, consisting of men and women who were born after Partition and Independence, and whose earliest childhood memories and experiences therefore go back at most to the 1950s. These 'children of *Midnight's Children*' have grown up in a country which is separated by a massive rupture from the India of the Raj, the larger 'India' that writers born before 1947—who dominate this anthology—knew, discovered, portrayed, recovered, freed, changed, and even took for granted. For the new poets and story-tellers, the individual opportunities, family situations, social practices, economic and political conditions, and cultural institutions that constitute 'everyday reality' are radically different: colonial India is at best a story, a discourse, an imagined or imaginary homeland, and the post-colonial India they know has barely begun to be charted. The best-known figures of this generation at present—Vikram Seth, Amitav Ghosh, Allan Sealy, and Upamanyu Chatterjee in prose and fiction, and Seth, Agha Shahid Ali, Meena Alexander, and Sujata Bhatt in verse—write in English, publish their books in England and America, and receive generous praise from cosmopolitan international audiences. In the course of the next twenty or thirty years they and their counterparts in the Indian languages, functioning as both the sites and the instruments of a larger process of change, will once more alter our conceptions of what 'India' is and has been, 'of what is past, or passing, or to come'.

Notes to the Poems

KEDARNATH SINGH, 'On Reading a Love Poem' (p. 4)

sakhu: an important variety of tree in India, also known as shal or sal; its resin is used widely in pharmaceuticals and varnish; its wood and resin, like those of the deodar tree, have been used traditionally in fire rituals.

P. LANKESH, 'Mother' (p. 6)

Savitri, Sita, Urmila: 'ideal' women in ancient Indian literature, myth, and folklore.

Ramakrishna: Ramakrishna Paramhansa, the nineteenth-century spiritual master who became the guru of Swami Vivekanand and the principal figure in the Ramakrishna Mission movement.

GAGAN GILL, 'The Girl's Desire Moves Among Her Bangles' (p. 8)

In traditional Indian communities, especially in the north, a young woman starts wearing glass bangles when she gets married. When her husband dies, she commences her widowhood by ritually breaking the bangles on the threshold of her home; thereafter, she may not wear any jewellery, ornaments, or cosmetics. In this poem, Gill equates a woman's condition, when her husband is unfaithful to her, to the condition of widowhood.

RABINDRANATH TAGORE, 'Flute-music' (p. 9)

Dacca sari: an expensive, highly-prized sari sometimes with gold-thread adornment, often used as a wedding-dress for a bride in Bengal.

vermilion: sindoor (in Hindi), a mineral-powder cosmetic which Hindu women apply everyday in the parting of their hair and as a bindi (spot) on their foreheads, to signify their married status. Traditionally, unmarried girls or women and widows do not use sindoor; it is first applied to a woman by her husband during the wedding ritual.

B.S. Mardhekar, 'The Forest of Yellow Bamboo Trees' (p. 25)

Polestar, Seven Sages: In Hindu mythology, the polestar is Dhruva, the archetype of mental, moral, and spiritual steadfastness, and the Great Bear represents a group of seven sages, who have to solve a riddle that Dhruva has posed.

Radha and Krishna: in the Hindu (Vaishnava) erotic tradition, the ideal pair of lovers, with Krishna as God or the divine object of Radha's human desire. In certain Vaishnava sects, however, Radha herself is also divine.

Padma Sachdev, 'The Well' (p. 35)

From a traditional Hindu viewpoint, the well is polluted and should not be used. For someone to drink from the well is to defy long-standing convention and ritual authority; for a woman (like the speaker in the poem) to do so is to be emphatically defiant, rebellious, and anti-conventional, particularly if she does it, not in darkness or in private, but in public and in broad daylight.

Sitanshu Yashashchandra, 'Drought' (p. 36)

In Gujarat, a well at a family home often has carved animal figures—such as the tortoise, the fish, or the cheetah—mounted down its sides to indicate how much water still remains in it. This poem revolves around the fact that, in the hot season and during a drought, as the water level in such a well falls steadily, it exposes successively lower carved figures on the inner wall.

Chandrashekhar Kambar, 'A Pond Named Ganga' (p. 41)

Birappa, Black Mother Goddess: in the Kannada-speaking countryside, common male and female folk deities, respectively.

Hundred Names, Thousand Names: especially in the tradition of the Puranas, the multiple 'holy names' (whether 108 or 1008) given to a deity; used by devotees and worshippers in various acts of prayer, devotion, and ritual.

Karna: in the *Mahabharata*, the noble and heroic 'illegitimate' son of a *shudra* charioteer (also allegorized as the sun) and Kunti (Pandu's elder wife and the mother of the first

three Pandavas); often referred to in later Indian literature
as the archetypal 'bastard' or 'misbegotten one'.

ANURADHA MAHAPATRA, 'Spell' (p. 47)

sacred banyan leaf: for more than two millenniums, Bud-
dhists (and Hindus) have treated the banyan as a sacred
tree, and associated it with religious or spiritual
'enlightenment'.

MRINAL PANDE, 'Two Women Knitting' (p. 47)

Rama and Uma: common, even stereotypical names for
women (housewives) of the first post-colonial generation in
the Hindi-speaking region.

INDIRA SANT, 'Household Fires' (p. 48)

five tongues of flame: metaphorically, the two daughters,
the two sons, and the husband of the housewife-mother
dramatized in the poem.

NIRENDRANATH CHAKRABARTI, 'Amalkanti' (p. 52)

Jaam, jaamrul: These are large, leafy fruit trees that grow in
Bengal. 'Jaam' is a fruit of the plum family.

KAMALA DAS, 'Hot Noon in Malabar' (p. 63)

kurava: an untouchable caste of fowlers, basket-makers, and
fortune-tellers in Kerala.

N. BALAMANI AMMA, 'To My Daughter' (p. 63)

daughter: the poet Kamala Das.

V. INDIRA BHAVANI, 'Avatars' (p. 66)

avatars: in ancient and post-classical Hindu mythology, the
ten avatars or incarnations of Vishnu; in classical and bhakti
poetry, a dashavatar poem praised the ten avatars of Vishnu,
whereas this poem satirically reduces the 'divine' avatars to
'profane' personality-traits in an unfaithful man.

SRI SRI, from 'Some People Laugh, Some People Cry' (p. 81)

Harishchandra: seventh-century Hindu king, often
regarded as an ideal (incorruptible) ruler.

rudraksha : a tree, the small round red fruit of which is dried and used as a bead on a 'rosary' for *japa,* the ritual act of remembering and quietly intoning a formula or a god's name; the bead is especially prized by worshippers of Shiva, who consider it 'supremely holy'.

SHRIKANT VERMA, 'The Pleasure Dome' (p. 86)

pleasure dome: a house or building designed for celebrations, festivals, parties; here used satirically.

China, Pakistan: references to the territorial wars India fought with these two neighbours in 1962 and 1965, respectively.

Surdas, Mathura: Surdas was the blind poet in the Braj language (a major literary 'dialect' of Hindi), who lived near the city of Mathura around the sixteenth century and wrote poems praising Lord Krishna as a child-god; here, Surdas and his poetry of 'salvation through love' are objects of ridicule.

salamander oil: commonly regarded as a substance which, when applied externally, restores and increases male sexual prowess.

Shiva's bow, suitors' contest: in the *Ramayana,* Rama participates in a suitors' contest in King Janaka's court, in which each contestant has to try and lift a giant, extremely heavy bow belonging to Lord Shiva; Rama succeeds in lifting, stretching, and breaking the bow, and thus wins Sita's hand in marriage.

G. SHANKARA KURUP, 'The Master Carpenter' (p. 91)

champak : a tree prized for its wood, fragrance, and aromatic flowers.

pandal : a large decorated tent or marquee, usually erected for weddings, festivals, or public functions.

Lakshmi: the goddess of wealth and good fortune, consort of Lord Vishnu.

SUJATA BHATT, 'What Is Worth Knowing?' (p. 99)

keema : a spicy minced-meat dish.

KAA NAA SUBRAMANYAM, 'Situation' (p. 101)

Max Mueller Bhavan: the cultural information centre and library set up in India by the West German government, with branches in several cities; named after the nineteenth-century German Indologist, Friedrich Max Müller.

Bowers, Danielou, Pope: Orientalist scholars who wrote 'classic' works on various Indian literatures, works, and art forms.

AMRITA PRITAM, 'The Creative Process' (p. 102)

karva chauth : among most north-Indian Hindus (especially Vaishnavas), a daylong fast kept once a year—on the fourth day after the full moon preceding the day of Diwali—by married women for the well-being of their husbands; the fast is broken at the first sighting of the moon in the evening.

RAGHUVIR SAHAY, 'Our Hindi' (p. 105)

Tulsidas: major sixteenth century Avadhi poet, author of the *Ramacharitmanas,* a *bhakti* retelling of the *Ramayana.*

Radheshyam: a popular modern reteller of the Rama story.

'Nagin': an very popular 'classic' Hindi film, a major box-office hit in the 1960s.

Kokshastra: a Sanskrit-style sex-manual.

Khari Baoli: a thirteenth-century settlement in north Delhi, now primarily a low-price printers' neighbourhood and a centre of 'yellow journalism'.

Bhavan: house, mansion.

BAHINABAI CHAUDHARI, 'The Naming of Things' (p. 107)

Hari: ancient name for God, used especially for Vishnu in his most general divine aspect.

KHALI-UR-RAHMAN AZMI, 'I and "I" ' (p. 112)

submission: the literal meaning of the Arabic word *islam.*

CHENNAVIRA KANAVI, 'On Bismillah Khan's Shehnai' (p. 115)

shehnai : Indian wind instrument of 'hypnotic power'; in

popular culture, its music is now associated strongly with Hindu wedding ceremonies and celebrations.

Bismillah Khan: the greatest modern master of the *shehnai*, who played it in the north Indian classical style.

BISHNU DE, 'Santhal Poems, 1' (p. 125)

A Bengali adaptation of a folksong of the people of the Santhal tribe in eastern India.

N. PICHAMURTI, 'National Bird' (p. 128)

national bird: the peacock.

specific: a remedy for a particular ailment.

BUDDHADEVA BOSE, 'Frogs' (p. 131)

The poem alludes throughout to the famous hymn about frogs in the *Rg-veda*, which satirizes brahmanical learning.

rishi : a sage or seer, a spiritual 'renouncer' and visionary (usually in ancient Indian myth and literature).

shloka : a metrical couplet in Sanskrit, used frequently in Vedic, epic, and classical Indian poetry.

SUNIL GANGOPADHYAY, 'Calcutta and I' (p. 135)

Jadu, Madhu, Shyam: The three names function together as a phrase synonymous with the English 'Tom, Dick and Harry'.

GHULAM MOHAMMED SHEIKH, 'Jaisalmer, 1' (p. 142)

Jaisalmer: a major historical town in western Rajasthan.

odhni : a woman's cotton wrap, draped over the head and around the torso.

chundadi : a woman's red garment, a wedding dress.

R. PARTHASARATHY, 'Speaking of Places' (p. 142)

Srirangam: 'the holy island', one of the holiest shrines of devotional Hinduism. The temple of Vishnu, who is called Ranganatha ('the lord of the island') there, is situated on an island in the River Kaveri.

bhaja govindam: 'worship Krishna', a phrase from one of Shankara's hymns.

Kashi: 'the city of light', Banaras, the oldest and holiest Hindu city. The temple of Shiva, who is called Vishvanatha ('the lord of the universe') there, is located on the right bank of the Ganga.

SHAMSHER BAHADUR SINGH, 'On the Slope of this Hill' (p. 145)
Jabalpur: an important city on the River Narmada in central India, in the state of Madhya Pradesh.

UMASHANKAR JOSHI, 'Passing through Rajasthan' (p. 146)
Padmini: a beautiful young Hindu princess of Chittor, who committed *jauhar* (ritual self-immolation) in order to escape from the Muslim sultan of Delhi, Alauddin Khalji, when the latter overran the famous walled city in southern Rajasthan.

CHEMMANAM CHACKO, 'Rice' (p. 148)
The poem plays on the differences between wheat-based cultures (symbolized by the chapati) and rice-based cultures which traditionally divide north India and south India, respectively.
modan, vellaran, athikira : common varieties of rice in Kerala.
Centre: in bureaucratic language, New Delhi, the capital of independent India.

NARAYAN SURVE, 'Lifetime' (p. 159)
four pillars: metaphorically, the four *varnas* (*brahman, kshatriya, vaishya, shudra*) in the Hindu caste system.

NAMDEO DHASAL, 'Stone-Masons, My Father, and Me' (p. 160)
stone-masons: in the original, *vadari*, an untouchable caste of migrant workers in the road-building and construction industries, whose members specialize in working with stone.
Parsi: in the poem, the Parsi is a representative of the capitalist class.

DOM MORAES, 'Babur' (p. 161)
Babur: the founder of the Mughal empire in India, who arrived in Delhi in 1526; the historical details in the poem are taken from Babur's Turkish memoirs.

K. NISAR AHMAD, 'America, America' (p. 167)

PL480: the number assigned by the U.S. Congress to its aid-package program for India, which started in 1955.

JYOTI LANJEWAR, 'I Never Saw You' (p. 171)

Lanjewar is a Maharashtrian Dalit woman writer, and here develops a poetic biography of her mother.

Gang of workers: among former untouchables who work in the road-building and construction industries, the women mostly carry gravel, sand, mortar, and concrete in wicker baskets or metal platters on their heads, between various points on the site. Such women labourers usually take their infants and young children to work with them, and often work during pregnancy.

Ambedkar: Dr B.R. Ambedkar, a member of the Constituent Assembly of India and one of the authors of the Indian Constitution; the leader of the movement in Maharashtra among untouchables to resist and undo caste-discrimination. Referred to later in the poem as 'Babasaheb' and 'Bhima'.

bhakri : a coarse, round, unleavened bread made fresh daily with the flour of jowar, bajra, or other inexpensive grain.

The Long March: organized by the followers of Dr Ambedkar, it took place in Maharashtra in 1956. It was part of the movement which resulted in the mass-conversion of about three million Maharashtrian untouchables to Buddhism in late 1956 and early 1957. After the event, the converts stopped using their traditional Hindu untouchable-caste names, and adopted the label 'Dalit', meaning 'ground down, oppressed'. Over the years, many Dalit protest marches and political rallies have ended in violence and police brutality.

Bhima: refers simultaneously to Dr Ambedkar and the character in the Mahabharata, who was physically the strongest and most heroic of the five Pandavas. Bhima is thus a ubiquitous double symbol of power, strength, resilience, tenacity, and heroic struggle in Dalit writing. 'Jai Bhima' means 'Victory to Bhima'.

Nirala, 'The Betrayal' (p. 177)

> *mridanga, tabla*: Indian classical percussion instruments, the first used mainly in the south and the second mainly in the north; the *mridanga* is a single drum with two faces, while the *tabla* consists of a pair of drums.
>
> *vina, surbahar*: Indian classical string instruments.
>
> spinet: a compact upright piano.

Suggestions for Further Reading

Readers who are unfamiliar with modern Indian poetry and wish to explore it further may find the following books, articles and periodicals useful.

Bahuvachan (Bhopal, 1988–)

Buddhadeva BOSE, ed., *An Anthology of Bengali Writing* (Madras: Macmillan, 1971)

David CEVET, ed., *The Shell and the Rain: Poems from New India* (London: George Allen & Unwin, 1973)

Chandrabhaga (Cuttack, 1978–)

Chelsea (New York), 46 (1987)

Chicago Review (Chicago), 38, nos. 1–2 (Spring 1992)

Dilip CHITRE, ed., *An Anthology of Marathi Poetry, 1945–65* (Bombay: Nirmala Sadanand, 1967)

Daedalus (Boston), 118, no. 4 (1989)

Vinay DHARWADKER, 'Twenty-nine Modern Indian Poems', *Tri-Quarterly* (Evanston, Illinois), 77 (Winter 1989–90): pp. 119–228

Vinay DHARWADKER, Barbara Stoler MILLER, A.K. RAMANUJAN and Eric A. HUBERMAN, 'Indian Poetry', in *The New Princeton Encyclopedia of Poetry and Poetics*, ed. Alex Preminger *et al.* (Princeton, New Jersey: Princeton University Press, 1993), pp. 585–600

Edward C. DIMOCK, Jr., *The Sound of Silent Guns* (Delhi: Oxford University Press, 1986)

Edward C. DIMOCK, Jr. and others, *The Literatures of India: An Introduction* (Chicago: University of Chicago Press, 1974)

Bruce KING, *Modern Indian Poetry in English* (Delhi: Oxford University Press, 1987)

———, *Three Indian Poets: Nissim Ezekiel, A.K. Ramanujan, Dom Moraes* (Madras: Oxford University Press, 1991)

Indian Literature (New Delhi, 1952–). Silver Jubilee issue, 23, nos. 3–4 (1980)

Indian Poetry Today, 4 vols. (New Delhi: Indian Council for Cultural Relations, 1974–81)

Journal of South Asian Literature (Rochester, Michigan, 1968–)

Adil JUSSAWALLA, ed., *New Writing in India* (Harmondsworth: Penguin, 1974)

Arvind Krishna MEHROTRA, ed., *The Oxford India Anthology of Twelve Modern Indian Poets* (Delhi: Oxford University Press, 1992)

Vidya Niwas MISRA, ed., *Modern Hindi Poetry* (Bloomington: Indiana University Press, 1965)

Meenakshi MUKHERJEE, ed., *Another India* (New Delhi: Penguin, 1990)

Nimrod (Tulsa, Oklahoma), 31, no. 2 (1988)

R. PARTHASARATHY, ed., *Ten Twentieth Century Indian Poets* (Delhi: Oxford University Press, 1976)

Poetry (Chicago), 93, no. 4 (January 1959)

Poetry India (Bombay, 1966–67)

David RAY and Amritjit SINGH, ed., *India: An Anthology of Contemporary Writing* (Athens, Ohio: Swallow Press, Ohio University Press, 1983)

David RUBIN, trans., *A Season on the Earth: Selected Poems of Nirala* (New York: Columbia University Press, 1976).

Karine SCHOMER, *Mahadevi Varma and the Chhayavad Age of Modern Hindi Poetry* (Berkeley: University of California Press, 1983)

Clinton B. SEELY, *A Poet Apart: A Literary Biography of the Bengali Poet Jibanananda Das (1899–1954)* (Newark: University of Delaware Press, 1990)

Rabindranath TAGORE, *Selected Poems*, trans. William Radice (Harmondsworth: Penguin, 1985)

Susie THARU and K. LALITA, ed., *Women Writing in India*, 2 vols. (New Delhi: Oxford University Press, 1993)

The Massachusetts Review (Amherst, Massachusetts), 29, no. 4 (1989)

Toronto South Asia Review (Toronto, Canada, 1987–)

Vagartha (New Delhi, 1974–79)

Shrikant VERMA, ed., *Poetry Festival India* (New Delhi: Indian Council for Cultural Relations, 1985)

World Literature Today (Norman, Oklahoma), special issue on 'Indian Literatures: In the Fifth Decade of Independence', 68, no. 2 (Spring 1994)

Select Notes on Poets and Translators

M. GOPALAKRISHNA ADIGA, who was born in 1918, taught English in Mysore and Udipi, and served as the principal of Lal Bahadur College, Sagar. He edited *Sakshi*, a literary magazine that started in 1967, and translated Ibsen and Whitman into Kannada. His books include *Bhavataranga* (1946), *Bhumigita* (1958), *Vardhamana* (1972), and *Idana Bayasiralilla* (1975), all collections of poetry; *Anathe*, a novel; and *Mannina vasane*, a volume of essays. English translations of his poems, by A.K. Ramanujan and M.G. Krishnamurthi, are available in *The Song of the Earth and Other Poems* (1968). Among his honours were a fellowship at the Institute of Advanced Study at Simla, the B.M.S. gold medal for poetry from Mysore University, and the Karnataka state Sahitya Akademi award. He received the Kabir Samman shortly before his death in 1992.

AGYEYA was the pen-name of Sachidananda Hirananda Vatsyayan, who was born in Kasia, Deoria, in Uttar Pradesh in 1911. In 1930–4 he was jailed by the British Indian government for revolutionary activity, and in 1942–6 he was in active service in World War II. Between the mid-1930's and mid-1980's he worked mainly as a journalist, editor, and teacher. Among other magazines and media publications, he edited *Pratik* (1946–52), *Dinman* (1964–9), *Naya Pratik* (1973–7), and *Navbharat Times* (1977–9). He also edited four anthologies of new Hindi poetry, the *Saptak* series (1943, 1951, 1959, 1979). He taught at Jodhpur University and, as a visiting professor, at the University of California, Berkeley. He published about two dozen books, including novels, plays, travel accounts, and collections of short stories, poems, and translations. His more recent poems are represented in *Kitani navon mein kitani bar* (1967) and *Sarjana ke kshana* (1979); in English translation they are available in *Nilambari* (1981). He received the national Sahitya Akademi award in 1964, and the Bharatiya Jnanapith award in 1978. Vatsyayan died in 1986.

AKHTAR-UL-IMAN was born into a priestly family in Qila, Najiba-bad, in the Bijnor District of Uttar Pradesh, in 1915. Brought up to become a priest, he ran away from home and was educated at a reform school with the help of an uncle. He received his B.A. from the Anglo-Arabic College, Delhi, and an M.A. from Aligarh Muslim University. Early in his career he worked for the Government of India and All India Radio. After 1945 he worked regularly as a dialogue writer, and occasionally as a director, in the Bombay film industry. Among his publications are a verse play and half a dozen books of poetry, including *Bint-e-lamhat* (1969) and *Naya ahang* (1977). His collection *Yaden* (1961) won the national Sahitya Akademi award in 1962.

MEENA ALEXANDER was born in Allahabad in 1951, into a family from Kerala. She was educated in India and England, and received a Ph.D. in literature from Nottingham University. She has worked at various colleges and universities in India and the United States, and currently teaches at Hunter College, New York. She has published literary and critical essays in English, as well as experimental prose fiction, short and long poems, and autobiographical writings. Her recent works are *House of a Thousand Doors* (1988), *The Storm* (1989), and *Night-Scene, the Garden* (1992).

AGHA SHAHID ALI, born in 1949, grew up in Delhi and Srinagar, Kashmir. He received an M.A. in English literature from the University of Delhi (1970), a Ph.D. in English from the Pennsylvania State University (1984), and an M.A. in creative writing from the University of Arizona (1985). He has taught English literature at Hindu College, Delhi, and currently teaches at the University of Massachusetts, Amherst. Among his recent publications are *The Rebel's Silhouette* (1991), trans-lations of Faiz Ahmed Faiz's selected Urdu poems; and *The Half-Inch Himalayas* (1987) and *A Nostalgist's Map of America* (1991), both collections of poems in English.

NALAPAT BALAMANI AMMA, or Balamani Nair, was born in Punna-yurkulam in Trichur, Kerala, in 1909. Between the early 1930's and the early 1980's, she published twenty books in Malayalam, including six of poetry. Her *Muthassi* (1962) won the Kerala state Sahitya Akademi award in 1964 and the national Sahitya Akademi award the following year. She received the title of Sahitya Nipuna from Tripunithura Sanskrit College in 1963. She is the mother of Kamala Das, also represented in this anthology.

KAIFI AZMI, whose real name is Athar Husain Rizvi, was born in Azamgarh, Uttar Pradesh, in 1924. In the 1940's he was an active member of the progressive writers' union, and an editor of *Naya adab*, a left-wing literary magazine. Since the 1950's he has been one of the major song writers in the Hindi film industry in Bombay. He is the father of actress and activist Shabana Azmi. His Urdu poems are collected in *Jhankar, Akhiri-shab*, and *Awara sajde*.

BAIDAR BAKHT, an engineer by profession, lives in Canada. He has extensively translated twentieth-century Urdu poetry from India and Pakistan with collaborators Leslie Lavigne and Kathleen Grant Jaeger. With Jaeger he has edited and translated *An Anthology of Modern Urdu Poetry* (1984) in two volumes.

HIRA BANSODE, born in 1939, has a master's degree in Marathi. She is one of the new Dalit women poets who became prominent in Maharashtra in the 1980's. She founded the Savadini Dalit Stree Sahitya Manch, and has been active in the subaltern women's movement for several years. Her two collections of poems are *Purnima* and *Fariyad*.

NIRMALPRABHA BARDOLOI, who was born in Sibsagar, Assam, in 1933, received her M.A. and Ph.D. degrees from Guwahati University. In the late 1950's she worked on the editorial staff of a newspaper and a monthly magazine, both published in Assamese. Since then she has been a teacher. Besides writing poetry and fiction for children, she has published essays on Assamese folk culture, and has written lyrics for films. Her volumes of poetry include *Dinar pachat din* (1977), *Samipesu* (1977), *Antaranga* (1978), and *Sudirgha din aru ritu*, which won the national Sahitya Akademi award in 1982.

DHIRENDRA NATH BEZBARUA has taught at the Regional College of Education, Mysore, and has served as the editor of *The Sentinel*, published from Guwahati, Assam. He has published

English translations of modern Assamese poetry regularly since the 1970's.

SUBRAMANIA BHARATI was born in Ettayapuram, Tamil Nadu, in 1882. When he was eleven, the Brahman scholars of his town awarded him the title 'Bharati' in recognition of his precocious gift for poetry and learning. Subsequently, between about 1900 and 1904, he was educated for a while in English at Hindu College, Tirunelvelli; lived briefly in Banaras; worked as a Tamil *pandit* in Madurai; and became a sub-editor of *Swadesha mitran,* a Tamil daily, in Madras. Between 1904 and 1907, largely because of his journalistic work and especially after his meeting with Sister Nivedita in 1905, he became a militant nationalist. In 1907, in response to his popular patriotic poems and anti-imperialist articles in the periodical *India,* the British colonial government issued a warrant for his arrest. Bharati fled to French Pondicherry, where he lived in poverty and hardship until 1918, but where he found the stimulating friendship of political exiles like Sri Aurobindo and V.V.S. Aiyar. In Pondicherry, he wrote what are called his 'three great poems,' *Kannan pattu, Panchati sapatham,* and *Kuyil pattu;* his prose poems and lyrics on Shakti; and his Tamil translations of Vedic hymns, Patanjali's *Yogasutras,* and the *Bhagavad-gita.* When Bharati returned to India in 1918, he was arrested at Cuddalore and imprisoned for three weeks, until Annie Besant and C.P. Ramaswamy Aiyar intervened on his behalf. Between then and 1920 he lived in Kadayam, by now sympathetic to Gandhi's non-violent freedom movement. He then accepted an invitation to return to the editorial staff of *Swadesha mitran,* where he worked until his death in 1921.

SUJATA BHATT was born in Ahmedabad in 1956 and grew up in Pune. Her family, originally from Gujarat, moved to the United States in the late 1960's. She studied creative writing at the University of Iowa, and now lives in Germany with her husband, Michael Augustin, a German writer. Her first book of poetry in English, *Brunizem* (1988), won the Alice Hunt Bartlett Prize in England, as well as the Commonwealth Poetry Prize for Asia. Her second collection, *Monkey Shadows,* was published in 1992. She translates Gujarati poetry into

English, and has also written experimental bilingual poems in English and Gujarati.

V. INDIRA BHAVANI, who also uses the pen-names Ivara and Indhu Varadhan, was born in Aruppukkottai, Tamilnadu, in 1942. She has published three collections of poetry in Tamil, as well as one volume of short stories.

BUDDHADEVA BOSE was born in 1908 and brought up in Dhaka, now in Bangladesh. He received his master's degree in English literature from Dhaka University, and started teaching at Ripon College, Calcutta, in 1934. The following year he launched the Bengali literary magazine *Kavita*, and in 1939 he founded Kavita Bhawan, both of which became major mid-century Bengali institutions, shaping the careers of other writers like Jibanananda Das, Samar Sen, Subhash Mukhopadhyay, and Naresh Guha. In 1954 Bose became the head of the Department of Comparative Literature at Jadavpur University, Calcutta, from where he retired at the end of the 1960's. He died in 1974. Over five decades, he published more than fifty books in Bengali and English, among them eleven books of poetry; thirteen novels; six collections of short stories; five plays; and eight volumes of literary criticism. Among his later books of poems were *Je adhar alor adhik* (1958), *Marchepada perekar gan* (1966), *Swagata biday* (1971), and *Ekdin chiradin* (1971). Bose was also an influential translator of Baudelaire, Rilke, Holderlin, and Kalidasa into Bengali; and an equally significant critic in works like *An Acre of Green Grass* (1946) and *Tagore: Portrait of a Poet* (1962).

NIRENDRANATH CHAKRABARTI was born in 1924 in Chandra, Faridpur district, now in Bangladesh. He received a B.A. from Calcutta University. He has been a journalist for more than three decades, writing for the *Ananda Bazar Patrika* between 1959 and 1976, and subsequently editing *Anandamela*, a children's magazine. Besides poetry in Bengali, he has published fiction as well as criticism. Among his various collections of poems, *Ulango raja* (1971) won the national Sahitya Akademi award in 1974. His other honours include the Tarashankar Literary Award in 1972, the Vidyasagar Lecturership at Calcutta University in 1975, and the Ananda Puraskar in 1976. His selected poems, translated by Sujit and Meenakshi Mukherjee, are available in *The Naked King and Other Poems* (1975).

AMIYA CHAKRAVARTY was born in 1901. Between 1926 and 1933 he worked as Rabindranath Tagore's literary secretary. He received a D.Phil. from Oxford University in 1938, and subsequently became a professor of comparative literature and religion in the United States. He returned to Shantiniketan, West Bengal, two years before his death in 1986. He wrote in Bengali as well as English. In the latter language he published a scholarly study of Thomas Hardy and an edited selection, *The Tagore Reader* (1961). His books of poetry in Bengali include *Khasra* (1937), *Parapar* (1959), and *Ghare pherar* (1961).

PRITHVINDRA CHAKRAVARTY was born in 1933 and educated at Shantiniketan, West Bengal, and the University of Chicago. He teaches at the University of Papua and New Guinea.

SHAKTI CHATTOPADHYAY was born in 1933 and educated at Presidency College, Calcutta. He has worked for the *Ananda Bazar Patrika*, the leading Bengali newspaper, for more than three decades. Together with the writers Sandipan Chattopadhyay and Utpal Basu, he started the Hungry Generation movement in Bengali writing in the early 1960's. Among his publications are about fifteen novels and books of poetry, as well as a translation of the *Rubaiyyat of Omar Khayyam*, and an edited anthology of Bengali poetry. He won the national Sahitya Akademi award in 1983 and has also been honoured with the Ananda Puraskar.

BAHINABAI CHAUDHARI was born in 1880 and died in 1951. She was an illiterate village woman who composed and transmitted her poems orally in the Khandeshi-Varhadi dialect of Marathi. Her songs were written down late in her lifetime by her son, Sopanadeo Chaudhari, who himself became a well-known poet. After her death, he showed the transcriptions of her songs to the prominent Marathi writer and journalist, Acharya Atre, who arranged for the publication of, and wrote an introduction to, *Bahinaichi gani* (1952).

DEVDAS CHHOTRAY, who was born in 1946, is a member of the Indian Administrative Service, and has published poetry in Oriya regularly since the 1970's.

DILIP PURUSHOTTAM CHITRE, born in 1938, grew up in Baroda and Bombay, and studied English literature at Bombay University. In the early 1960's, he lived and worked as a school teacher in Ethiopia. Since then he has lived in Bombay and Pune, among other places, and has worked in advertising and as an editor and free-lance writer. In the 1980's he also served as the director of Bharat Bhavan, Bhopal. He has published poetry, fiction, criticism, and travel and journalistic writing in English and Marathi, and has translated extensively from Marathi into English. His publications include *Travelling in a Cage* (1980), poems in English; *Kavite nantarchya kavita* (1978), poems in Marathi; and *An Anthology of Marathi Poetry, 1945–65* (1967) and *Says Tuka* (1991), both edited volumes of translations. Among his honours are the Maharashtra government poetry award in 1960–61, and the Karad Puraskar and the Godavareesh Memorial Award, both in 1981. He was a visitor at the Iowa International Writing Program in 1975–7.

CARLO COPPOLA is a scholar of Urdu and modern Indian literature, and of Islamic culture. He is a professor at Oakland University, Rochester, Michigan, from where he has edited *The Journal of South Asian Literature* for more than a dozen years. He has translated a large number of Urdu poems and stories in the past two decades, and is currently working on a study of Ahmed Ali.

KEKI NASSERWANJI DARUWALLA was born in 1937 into a Parsi family in Lahore, now in Pakistan. He received an M.A. in English from Government College, Punjab University, Ludhiana. He entered the Indian Police Service in the late 1950's, and worked for the Government of India for more than three decades, with postings in New Delhi, various northern states, and England. He has published prose fiction, essays, and book reviews in English, and has edited *Two Decades of Indian Poetry: 1960–1980* (1980), an anthology of Indian English verse. He has published half a dozen collections of poems, including *The Keeper of the Dead* (1982) and *Landscapes* (1987). He won the national Sahitya Akademi award for the former volume in 1984, and the Commonwealth Poetry Prize for Asia for the latter in 1987.

JAGANNATH PRASAD DAS, born in 1936, was educated at Allahabad University, and worked for several years in the Indian Administrative Service. Since the late 1960's he has published a dozen books, including collections of his poems and plays in Oriya, essays on the art and culture of Orissa, and translations of his own and other Oriya poets' work into English and other languages. Among his collections of poems are *Anya sabu mrityu* (1976) and *Je jahara nirjanta* (1978). His early selected poems in English translation are gathered in *Love Is a Season* (1978). Of his recent publications, *Under a Silent Sun* (1992) is an anthology of recent Oriya women poetry, translated and edited with Arlene Zide.

JIBANANANDA DAS, born into a devout Brahmo Samaj family in 1899, grew up in rural Barisal in undivided Bengal. He studied English literature for his M.A. at Calcutta University. He taught at various colleges in Calcutta, including City College, and also worked for some time on the editorial staff of the daily *Swaraj*. He died from the injuries he received when he was hit by a moving tramcar in Calcutta in October 1954. The following year the Sahitya Akademi awarded him its first annual prize for Bengali, posthumously for *Jibanananda Daser shreshtha kavita* (1955). Das belonged to the controversial school of 'pure' poetry and is now considered the most important poet in Bengali after Tagore. Among his other collections of poetry are *Dhusar pandulipi* (1936), *Banalata sen* (1942), and *Mahaprithvi* (1944); as well as the posthumously published *Rupasi bangla* (1957) and *Bela abela kalbela* (1961). His essays on poetry were collected after his death in *Kaviter katha* (1955).

KAMALA DAS was born in Punnayurkulam, Kerala, in 1934. She was educated at home by her mother, the Malayalam poet Balamani Amma. Das has published poetry, prose fiction, and autobiographical and journalistic writing in English as well as Malayalam. In the latter language, her work appears under her maternal grandmother's name, Madhavikutty. Her early English poems are collected in *Summer in Calcutta* (1965), *The Descendants* (1967), and *The Old Playhouse and Other Poems* (1973). Her autobiography, *My Story*, appeared in 1975, and her only novel in Malayalam, *Manasi*, was translated as *Alphabet of Lust* in 1978. Her honours include the P.E.N. Asian Poetry Prize in Manila in 1963, the Kerala state Sahitya Akademi award for short fiction in 1969, and the Chimanlal Prize for journalism in 1971 and 1986.

PRANABENDU DASGUPTA, who also writes under the pen-name Abhimanyu Sen, was born in Calcutta in 1937. He received a master's degree in comparative literature from Calcutta University and another in English from the University of North Carolina in the United States. He earned a Ph.D. in comparative literature from the University of Minnesota, and has been teaching in the Department of Comparative Literature at Jadavpur University, Calcutta, since the early 1970's. Among his half a dozen books are a novel for children, a play, and *Nijosya ghurir prati* (1975) and *Sudhu bicchinnata noi* (1976), both collections of poems.

JYOTIRMOY DATTA was born into a Bengali family in Murshidabad in 1936, and grew up in rural south India. He has worked as a journalist, editor, and teacher, writing for *The Statesman* during 1956–68, and editing *Kolkata*, a magazine. His poems, essays, and translations have appeared widely in English and Bengali. He has been a visitor at the University of Chicago as well as the Iowa International Writing Program.

BISHNU DE, born in Calcutta in 1909, received his bachelor's degree from Calcutta University. Between 1935 and 1969, he taught English literature in Calcutta, at Ripon College, Presidency College, and the former Central Calcutta College. He has published nearly forty books in Bengali and English, including Bengali translations from English, essays in English on art and aesthetics, and English translations of his own Bengali poems, the last in *History's Tragic Exultation* (1973). His *Smriti satta bhabisyat* (1963) won the national Sahitya Akademi award in 1965, and *Rushati panchasati* (1967) won the Soviet Land–Nehru award in 1969. *Bachhar panchise* (1973) brings together poems from eight earlier collections. He received the Bharatiya Jnanpith award in 1971.

EUNICE DE SOUZA was born in Pune in 1940, and educated there and at Sophia College, Bombay. She earned an M.A. in English from Marquette University, Wisconsin, and a Ph.D. from the University of Bombay. Since the late 1960's, she has taught at St Xavier College, Bombay, where she is now the head of the English Department. She has published criticism, book reviews, essays, children's books, and, with Adil Jussawalla, an edited anthology of Indian English prose, *Statements* (1976). Her collections of poems include *Women in Dutch Painting* (1988) and *Ways of Belonging: New and Selected Poems* (1990), the latter a Poetry Book Society Recommendation in England.

NABANEETA DEV SEN was born in Calcutta in 1938. Her parents were the Bengali writers Narendra Dev and Radharani Debi (who also wrote under the pen-name Aparajita Debi). She was educated at Presidency College, Calcutta, and subsequently received her M.A. and Ph.D. degrees in comparative literature from Harvard University and Indiana University, Bloomington, respectively. She married the economist Amartya Sen and they lived in England for many years. When the marriage ended, she returned with her two daughters to Calcutta, where she became professor of comparative literature at Jadavpur University, a position she still holds. She has more than twenty books to her credit in Bengali and English, among them novels, travelogues, and fiction for children, and collections of poems, short stories, and literary and critical essays. Her volumes of poetry in Bengali include *Prathama pratyay* and *Swagat devaduta.* Among her recent books are *Nati nabaneeta* (1983), a volume of essays, and *Sit sahasit hemontalok* (1990), a novel. She has been a visiting scholar and professor at several universities in England and the United States, including Oxford, Harvard, and Columbia.

IMTIAZ DHARKER was born in Lahore, Pakistan, in 1954. She has an M.A. in philosophy from Glasgow University, and has lived in Bombay since the 1970's. She is an artist as well as a poet in English, and for several years was the poetry editor of *Debonair*. Her poems are collected in *Purdah* (1992).

APARNA DHARWADKER was born in Jaipur, Rajasthan, in 1956, and educated there and in Delhi. She received her Ph.D. from the Pennsylvania State University in 1990. She has taught English literature at Hindu College, Delhi; the University of Illinois, Chicago; and the University of Georgia. She is currently an assistant professor of drama and Restoration and eighteenth-century literature at the University of Oklahoma, Norman. She has published translations of Hindi poems by Shrikant Verma and Kunwar Narain, and essays on plays by Girish Karnad, P.L. Deshpande, and Wole Soyinka.

VINAY DHARWADKER was born in Pune, Maharashtra, in 1954, and educated in New Delhi and Jaipur. He attended St. Stephen's College, and received a B.Sc. and an M.Sc. in physics from the University of Delhi. Between 1976 and 1981 he worked as an editor at Orient Longman, New Delhi. He moved to the United States in 1981, and received a Ph.D. in South Asian studies from the University of Chicago. Between 1989 and 1991 he was assistant professor of Commonwealth literatures at the University of Georgia. He currently teaches modern British and American literature, Indian and world literatures, and literary theory at the University of Oklahoma. His books include *Sunday at the Lodi Gardens* (1994), a volume of poems in English, and *The Columbia Book of Indian Poetry*, an edited anthology (forthcoming). A selection of his translations of contemporary Hindi and Marathi poems appeared in 1990 as a book-length special feature in *Tri Quarterly*, no. 77.

NAMDEO DHASAL was born probably in 1949, and grew up in the slums of Bombay. He was educated up to the high school level in Marathi. In 1972 he and Raja Dhale, another Dalit writer, formed the Dalit Panthers, a group that attracted national and international attention for its militant anti-caste politics. For about a decade after the mid-1970's, Dhasal was associated with several other political groups, including the more radical communists and the youth wing of the Congress (I) Party. His early poetry is collected in *Golpitha* (1974) and *Murkha mhataryane dongara halavale* (1975).

DHOOMIL was the pen-name of Sudama Pandeya, who was born in a village near Varanasi in 1935, and died in that city in 1975. He taught electrical engineering at an industrial institute there, and published one collection of poems in his lifetime, *Sansad se sadak tak* (1972). His later poems were collected and published posthumously in *Kal sunana mujhe* (1977).

PHILIP C. ENGBLOM has studied Marathi in India and the United States, and has taught at various colleges since the 1980's. His publications include essays on Marathi and Indian literature, as well as translations of modern Marathi poetry and prose. Among the latter are versions of poems by P.S. Rege and Bahinabai Chaudhari; stories by D.B. Mokashi, G.A. Kulkarni, and Gauri Deshpande; and a book-length work, *Palkhi* (1986), Mokashi's classic account of the Varkari pilgrimage to Pandharpur in the 1960's.

NISSIM EZEKIEL was born into a Bene-Israeli family in Bombay in 1924. He was educated at Wilson College, Bombay, and Birbeck College, London. In the 1950's he worked in journalism, broadcasting, and advertising in Bombay, before becoming a college teacher of English and American literature. He has taught at Mithibai College of Arts, Bombay, and as a visiting professor at Leeds University. He retired in the mid-1980's as professor of English at the University of Bombay. He has published plays, art criticism, newspaper columns, and book-reviews. As an editor, he has been associated with *Quest, Imprint, Poetry India,* and *The Indian P.E.N.* His recent books are *Collected Poems* (1989) and *Selected Prose* (1992). He received the national Sahitya Akademi award in 1982, and the Government of India's Padma Shri award in 1988.

SUNIL GANGOPADHYAY was born in Faridpur—now in Bangladesh—in 1934, and received his master's degree from Calcutta University. He has been a journalist by profession, and has worked on the editorial staff of the *Ananda Bazar*

Patrika for well over two decades. He has published more than one hundred books of fiction and poetry in Bengali, including two classic modern Bengali novels, *Aranyer din ratri* (1969) and *Pratidwandi* (1970), both made into films by Satyajit Ray. His honours include the Ananda Puraskar.

GAGAN GILL, born in New Delhi in 1959, received an M.A. in English from the University of Delhi. She is married to the Hindi novelist Nirmal Verma and lives in New Delhi. She works as a journalist in Hindi and Punjabi, and has been the literary editor of the Hindi *Sunday Observer* and the Hindi editor of the *Telegraph*. Her first collection of poems, *Ek din lautegi ladaki*, appeared in 1989. She was a visitor at the Iowa International Writing Program in 1989–90.

NARESH GUHA was born in Tangail, now in Bangladesh, in 1924. He was educated at Calcutta University, and at Northwestern University, Illinois. He worked as an editor for Signet Press in Calcutta, between 1948 and 1956, and as an assistant editor of *Kavita*, the leading Bengali poetry magazine, between 1954 and 1960. After 1967, until his retirement, he was professor of comparative literature at Jadavpur University, Calcutta. His dozen books include a scholarly study of W.B. Yeats in English; edited collections in Bengali of the poetry of Amiya Chakravarty and Buddhadeva Bose; and collections of his own Bengali short stories and poems, among the latter being *Tatar samudra ghera* (1976).

POPATI RAMCHAND HIRANANDANI was born in Hyderabad, Sind (now in Pakistan), in 1924, and was educated at Banaras Hindu University. She has been a scholar, critic, and teacher of Sindhi, and retired as the head of the Sindhi Department, K.C. College, Bombay. She has over twenty publications to her credit, including a novel, an autobiography, a philological study of the Sindhi language, and collections of poems, short stories, essays, and humorous pieces. She won the national Sahitya Akademi award in 1982.

ALI SARDAR JAFRI was born in Balrampur, Uttar Pradesh, in 1913. He received his B.A. from the Anglo-Arabic College, Delhi, and was very closely identified with the Progressive Writers' Movement from the 1930's onwards. He has worked as a journalist, editor, and television producer. He has published half a dozen collections of poems in Urdu, and several works of prose in Urdu and English. His honours include the Padma Shri in 1967, the Soviet Land–Nehru award, the Mir Taqi Mir prize, and the Bhopal Urdu Academy prize.

A. JAYAPRABHA was born in Nagpur, Maharashtra, in 1957, but grew up in Vishakapatnam, Andhra Pradesh, where her family moved after her father's retirement. She has a Ph.D. in Telugu literature. She is married to the young Telugu poet Suryanarayana, and they published their first book together, *Suryudu kuda udayistadu* (1980). Since then she has published two books of literary criticism and five collections of poetry, among the latter *Vamanudi mudopadam* (1988) and *Kurisina varsham ekkadi meghanidi* (1992). She edits, with K. Satyavathy, the Telugu feminist monthly magazine *Lohita*. In 1989–90 she was a visiting scholar at the University of Wisconsin, Madison.

UMASHANKAR JETHALAL JOSHI was born in Bamana, Gujarat, in 1911, and received his M.A. from the University of Bombay in 1938. He was a professor of Gujarati at Gujarat Vidya Sabha, Ahmedabad, in 1939–46. Between the late 1940's and the early 1970's, he served as a professor of Gujarati, as the director of the School of Languages, and as Vice-Chancellor at the University of Gujarat. He was a nominated member of the Rajya Sabha, the upper house of Indian Parliament, during 1970–6, Vice President, Indian P.E.N., and Chairman, Indian Institute of Mass Communication, during 1978–80. He also served as the president of the Sahitya Akademi in New Delhi, and Acharya (Chancellor) of Vishwa-Bharati. He edited *Sanskriti*, which was a monthly magazine between 1946 and 1980, and has been a quarterly since then. Between the early 1930's and the early 1980's, he published about forty books, including translations, a novel, collections of short fiction and one-act plays and edited collections, and several works of literary criticism. His poetry is collected in *Samagra kavita 1931–81* (1981). His honours include the Bharatiya Jnanapith award in 1967; the Sahitya Akademi award in 1973; the Soviet Land–Nehru award in 1979; and the Mahakavi Kumaran Asan prize in 1982.

ADIL JEHANGIR JUSSAWALLA was born into a Parsi family in Bombay
in 1940, and educated there and at University College, Ox-
ford. Between the late 1950's and the end of the 1960's he
lived in England. In the early 1970's he taught English
literature at St Xavier's College, Bombay, and since then has
been working for various newspapers and magazines in the
city. He has published literary and art criticism as well as
literary essays and prose fiction in English. His books include
New Writing in India (1974), an edited anthology of post-
Independence Indian writing in English and in translation
from the major languages; *Statements* (1976), an anthology
of Indian English prose, edited with Eunice de Souza; and
Missing Person (1976), a collection of poems in English.

CHENNAVIRA SAKRAPPA KANAVI was born in Hombal, Dharwar
district, Karnataka, in 1928. He earned an M.A. from Kar-
nataka University, and was the director of the extension
service and university publications there. Among his two
dozen books are works of criticism and volumes of poetry,
the latter including *Nela-mugilu* (1965), which won a Mysore
Government award in 1966, and *Jivadhvani* (1980), which
received the national Sahitya Akademi award in 1981.

VINDA KARANDIKAR was born in 1918 in a village in Ratnagiri
district, in the Konkan region of Maharashtra. He was edu-
cated at Rajaram College, Kolhapur, and at the University
of Bombay, receiving an M.A. in English in 1946. He taught
literature for more than thirty years in Bombay, retiring
from S.I.E.S. College in the 1980's. He was a senior Fulbright
fellow and a visiting scholar at the University of Chicago in
1967–8, and participated in the Pushkin poetry festival in
the U.S.S.R. in 1970. He has published over twenty books,
among which are collections of poems, children's verse, and
essays and criticism, as well as Marathi translations of
Aristotle's *Poetics*, Goethe's *Faust* (Part One), and
Shakespeare's *King Lear*. His selected Marathi poems are
available in *Samhita* (1975), and his own English translations
of his poems are gathered in *Poems of Vinda* (1975), *Trimurti*
(1979), and *Some More Poems of Vinda* (1983). His honours
include several Maharashtra state awards, including the

Keshavsut poetry prize; the Soviet Land–Nehru award (1970); the Mahakavi Kumaran Asan prize (1982); and the Kabir Samman (1992).

ARUN BALKRISHNA KOLATKAR was born in Kolhapur in 1932 and received his early education there. Subsequently he studied art in Bombay and Pune, receiving a diploma from the J.J. School of Art, Bombay, in 1957. Since then he has worked mainly in advertising, and has won national professional awards for his work. Since the mid-1950's he has published poetry in English and Marathi, as well as English translations of Marathi poetry. His books are *Jejuri* (1976), a long sequence of poems in English, and *Arun kolatkarchya kavita* (1977), collected poems in Marathi. The former won the Commonwealth Poetry Prize, and the latter received the Maharashtra government poetry prize.

SATI KUMAR, who was born in 1938 and writes in both Hindi and Punjabi, has published several volumes of poetry in the latter language. He has lived in Europe for many years, and has translated Indian poetry into Bulgarian.

SHIV K. KUMAR was born in Lahore, now in Pakistan, in 1921. He was educated there at Forman Christian College, and at Fitzwilliam College, Cambridge. He taught for many years at the University of Delhi and the University of Hyderabad, and was a visiting professor at various British and American universities and colleges in the 1970's and 1980's. He has published scholarly criticism, prose fiction, a play, as well as poetry in English. His books of poetry include *Cobwebs in the Sun* (1976). Among his honours are a Cultural Award visit to Australia in 1971, and election as a fellow of the Royal Society of Literature in 1974.

JYOTI BABURAE LANJEWAR was born in Nagpur, Maharashtra, in 1950. She has a Ph.D. in Marathi, and teaches in Aurangabad. She has published four books, including *Disha*, a collection of poems.

P. LANKESH, was born in Konagavalli, Shimoga district, Karnataka, in 1935. He earned his M.A. in English literature from Mysore University in 1959. He has taught at the University of Bangalore, has produced and directed films, and has worked as an editor and journalist, publishing his own newspaper, *Lankesh patrike*. Besides translating Sophocles and Baudelaire into Kannada, he has published nearly twenty books of poetry, short and novelistic fiction, and drama, as well as an edited anthology of modern Kannada poetry. His collections of poems in Kannada include *Bicchu* (1967) and *Thalemaru* (1971).

ANURADHA MAHAPATRA was born in 1956 into a rural working-class family in West Bengal. She received an M.A. in Bengali literature from Calcutta University, and has served as an editorial assistant for *Kolkata 2000*. Her collection of poems *Chaiphulstup* appeared in 1983.

JAYANTA MAHAPATRA, born in Cuttack in 1928, was educated there and in Patna. He worked as a college teacher of physics in Orissa for more than thirty years, and retired from Ravenshaw College, Cuttack. He started writing poetry in English late in his thirties, and has published a dozen books since then. His recent works include *Selected Poems* (1987) and *The Temple* (1989). He has also published essays on poetry, and has extensively translated contemporary writing from Oriya into English. As an editor, he has been associated with *The Gray Book*, *Chandrabhaga*, and *Kavyabharati*, all literary magazines in English. He won the Jacob Glatstein Memorial prize from *Poetry* (Chicago) in 1975, and the national Sahitya Akademi award in 1981.

SITAKANT MAHAPATRA was born in 1937 and was educated at Allahabad University and at Cambridge University, England. He has been a member of the Indian Administrative Service in Orissa for over thirty years. He has published more than two dozen books in Oriya and English, among them collections of his Oriya poems, English translations of his own poetry, and several anthologies of Oriya tribal poems in English translation, among the last, *The Wooden Sword* (1973) and *Bakhen* (1979). He has also published collections of his essays in English on literature and culture, and has edited anthologies of English translations of Gopinath Mohanty's stories and of modern Oriya poetry. His more recent Oriya poetry is available in *Samudra* (1977), *Chitranadi* (1979), and

Drushya (1981); and his own English versions of his Oriya poems are collected in *The Song of Kubja and Other Poems* (1980), among other volumes. He has received the Orissa state Sahitya Akademi award, as well as the national Sahitya Akademi award. He won the Bharatiya Jnanpith award in 1993.

BENOY MAJUMDAR was born in 1934 into a Bengali family in Thedo, Myiktila district, Burma. His family moved to India in 1943, when the British army retreated before advancing Japanese forces. He received his bachelor's degree in engineering from Calcutta University, and later worked for a short time at a steel plant in Durgapur. During a period of unemployment he translated material from Russian into Bengali for the People's Publishing House. He was one of the young poets associated with the Hungry Generation movement in the early 1960's. He has published more than a dozen volumes of poetry in Bengali, including *Aghraner anubhutimala* (1974) and *Balmikir kabita* (1976).

BAL SITARAM MARDHEKAR was born in 1909 and educated in Pune, Maharashtra, and in England. He taught in various colleges in Maharashtra before joining All India Radio. He wrote in English and Marathi. In the former language, he published *Arts and the Man* (1941), a theoretical work on aesthetics. In Marathi, he published three experimental novels, *Ratricha divas* (1942), *Tambadi mati* (1943), and *Pani* (1948), as well as three collections of poems, *Sisirangama* (1939), *Kahi kavita* (1947), and *Ankhi kahi kavita* (1950). He died at the age of forty-seven in 1956.

R. MEENAKSHI was born in Virudhunagar, Tamil Nadu, in 1944. Since 1976 she has worked as an educational researcher at Auroville, the international township associated with the Sri Aurobindo ashram in Pondicherry. A teacher and social worker, she has published four books of her poetry in Tamil.

ARVIND KRISHNA MEHROTRA was born in 1947 in Lahore, Pakistan, and was educated at Allahabad University and the University of Bombay. He has taught at the University of Hyderabad, and is currently professor of English at Allahabad. He was a visitor at the Iowa International Writing Program in 1971–73. He has published poetry and criticism in English, as well as translations of poetry from Hindi and Prakrit. His recent books are *Middle Earth* (1984), a collection of new and selected poems, and *The Absent Traveller* (1991), a book of translations from Prakrit. He has edited *The Oxford India Anthology of Twelve Modern Indian Poets* (1992) and co-edited *Periplus*, a volume of and about poetry in translation (1993).

JYOTSNA MILAN, who comes from a Gujarati family, was born in Bombay in 1941. She has master's degrees in Gujarati and English literature, and writes in Gujarati and Hindi. Among her publications in Hindi are *Apne saath* (1976), a novel; *Cheekh ke aar paar* (1979), a volume of short stories; and *Ghar nahin* (1989), a book of poems. Her fiction is available in English translation in *Khandahar and Other Stories* (1982). She edits *Anasuya*, a women's journal published by Seva Bharat, an organization in Bhopal. She has translated the poems of Niranjan Bhagat, Suresh Joshi, Priyakant Maniyar, Ghulam Mohammed Sheikh, Labhshankar Thacker, and Sitanshu Yashashchandra from Gujarati into Hindi.

SOUBHAGYA KUMAR MISHRA, born in 1941, teaches English at Behrampur University, Orissa, and has published several collections of poetry in Oriya.

DOMINIC FRANK MORAES was born in 1938 in Bombay, and educated there and at Jesus College, Oxford. He has published thirty books in English, as well as a large quantity of journalistic writing. His prose works include biographies, travel accounts, coffee-table books, and an autobiography. His recent volumes of poetry are *Collected Poems* (1987) and *Serendip* (1990). He won the Hawthorndon Prize in England at the age of nineteen for his first collection of poems, *A Beginning* (1957).

MEENAKSHI MUKHERJEE is professor of English and head of the Department of English at the School of Languages, Jawaharlal Nehru University, New Delhi. She has taught at the University of Pune, Lady Shri Ram College (University of Delhi), the University of Hyderabad, and as a visiting professor at various American universities. She has written exten-

sively about Indian English, British, and British Common-
wealth literatures, as well as about modern literatures in
Bengali and other Indian languages. She has also translated
a large quantity of poetry and prose fiction from Bengali
into English, including works by Lokenath Bhattacharya.
Her books of criticism include *The Twice-born Fiction* (1971)
and *Realism and Reality* (1985). Between 1974 and 1980, she
edited *Vagartha*, a quarterly magazine of contemporary In-
dian literature in translation, published from New Delhi. A
selection from the volumes of *Vagartha* is available in *Another
India* (1990), edited by Nissim Ezekiel and Mukherjee.

SUJIT MUKHERJEE taught English literature at the University of
Pune before serving as the chief editor at Orient Longman,
in New Delhi and Hyderabad. He has published scholarly
articles and books on Indian literature and literary history,
and on the theory and practice of translation. He has also
translated extensively from modern Bengali verse and prose,
including works by Rabindranath Tagore, Amiya Chakravar-
ty, Nirendranath Chakrabarti, and Sunil Gangopadhyay.

SUBHASH MUKHOPADHYAY was born in 1919. He has been the
editor of *Parichay*, a Bengali literary monthly, and *Sandesh*,
a children's magazine, both published from Calcutta. His
book of poems, *Jato durei jai*, won the national Sahitya
Akademi award.

VIJAYA MUKHOPADHYAY was born in Vikrampur, now in Bangla-
desh, in 1937. She holds an M.A. in Sanskrit and teaches at
the Ramakrishna Sharada Mission College, Calcutta. She
edits *Bibhasha*, a Bengali literary magazine, translates from
and into Bengali, and appears frequently on radio and
television and at public readings. She has published seven
books of poetry in Bengali, among which are *Jodi shartahin*
(1971), *Bhenge jay anata badam* (1977), and *Udanta nan-
mabali*. She won the Kabi award of the Sara Bangla Kabi
Sammelan in 1974.

GAJANAN MADHAV MUKTIBODH was born in 1917 in Shiopur,
Madhya Pradesh, into a family that had recently migrated
from Maharashtra to the princely state of Gwalior. He was
educated in Gwalior and Ujjain, and received his bachelor's

degree from Holkar College, Indore, in 1938. At the end of the 1930's and early in the following decade he taught in schools in Ujjain and Shuljapur. Around this time he became an active and prominent member of the Progressive Writers' Union. Between 1945 and 1949 he worked as a journalist, editor, and broadcaster in Varanasi, Jabalpur, Nagpur, and Allahabad. He received an M.A. in 1954 and became a lecturer at Digvijay College, Rajnandgaon, a position he retained until he died of tubercular meningitis in 1964 at the age of forty-seven. Although his mother-tongue was Marathi, he wrote a large quantity of experimental poetry, short and novelistic fiction, and literary and social criticism in Hindi. His last poems were published posthumously in *Chand ka munh tedha hai* (1964), and his collected prose and verse is available in the multivolume *Muktibodh rachanavali* (1980).

MUNIB-UR-RAHMAN was born in Agra, Uttar Pradesh, in 1924. He received his M.A. from Aligarh Muslim University and his Ph.D. from the University of London, England. He has served as the director of the Islamic Studies Centre at Aligarh, and has taught in the Department of Modern Languages, Oakland University, Michigan. He is a scholar and translator of Persian poetry and Urdu literature, and has published scholarly work in Urdu and English. His books of poetry in Urdu appeared in 1965 and 1983.

C.M. NAIM was born in Barabanki, Uttar Pradesh, in 1934, and was educated in India and the United States. He has been a professor of Urdu and Islamic studies at the University of Chicago for almost three decades. He has edited *Mahfil* and its successor, *The Journal of South Asian Literature*, as well as *The Annual of Urdu Studies*. He has extensively translated modern Urdu poetry and fiction from India and Pakistan, and is currently working on an annotated translation of Mir's Persian autobiography, *Zikr-e-Mir*. Among his recent publications is an edited volume, *Iqbal, Jinnah, and Pakistan: The Vision and the Reality*.

NARA is the pen-name of Velcheru Narayana Rao, who was born in Ambakhandi, Andhra Pradesh, in 1932. He is a scholar, critic, and translator of Telugu literature, and teaches South Asian studies at the University of Wisconsin, Madison. His latest book is *When God Is a Customer* (1994), a selection of seventeenth-century Telugu courtesan songs by Kshetrayya and others, translated with David Shulman and A.K. Ramanujan. He was a Guggenheim Fellow in India in 1991–2.

KUNWAR NARAIN was born in Faizabad, Uttar Pradesh, in 1927, and received a master's degree in English literature from Lucknow University. He is a businessman by profession, and lives in Lucknow. His short stories are collected in *Akaron ke aas paas* (1971) and among his volumes of poetry are *Atmajayi* (1965) and *Apne samane* (1979). He has served as vice-chairman of the Uttar Pradesh Sangeet Natak Academy between 1976 and 1979, and as a member of the editorial board of *Naya pratik*, a monthly magazine edited by S.H. Vatsyayan, during 1975–8. His honours include the Hindustani Academy award for poetry in 1971 and the Uttar Pradesh government's Premchand Puraskar for fiction in 1972–3.

KIKKERI SUBBARAO NARASIMHASWAMI was born in Kikkeri, Mandya district, Karnataka, in 1915. He worked for the Karnataka state government for over thirty years. He published more than twenty books in Kannada between the early 1940's and the early 1980's, among them collections of essays and poems, the latter including *Tereda bagilu* (1976). He received the Karnataka Rajyotsava Award in 1972, the Karnataka state Sahitya Akademi prize in 1973, and the national Sahitya Akademi award for poetry in 1977.

NIRALA was the pen-name of Suryakant Tripathi, who was born in 1896 and died in 1961. He was one of the principal figures in the 'romantic' *chhayavad* and the progressive *pragativad* movements in Hindi literature between the 1920's and the 1950's. His collected works are available in the multivolume *Nirala rachanavali* (1983). His selected poems are translated by David Rubin in *A Season on the Earth* (1976).

MANGESH PADGAONKAR was born in Vengurla, Maharashtra, in 1929, and was educated in Bombay. He received his bachelor's degree, a teacher's diploma, and a master's degree in Marathi and Sanskrit from Kirti College, Bombay. Between 1958 and 1960 he worked as an assistant producer at All India Radio, Bombay. For the next five years he was a professor of Marathi, first at Somaiya College and then at Mithibai College. During 1965–70 he returned to All India Radio as a producer, and in 1970 he became a Marathi editor at the United States Information Service in Bombay, a position he held until his retirement in the late 1980's. Among his publications are a verse play, a book of essays and sketches, and a dozen collections of poetry, including *Vidushak* (1966), *Salaam* (1978), and *Ghazal* (1984). He received the national Sahitya Akademi award in 1980.

MRINAL PANDE, born in 1946 in Nainital, Uttar Pradesh, earned a master's degree in English from Allahabad University. She works in New Delhi as a journalist and editor, and is also associated with the broadcast media, writing and producing serials for television and appearing regularly on discussion programmes. She has edited *Vama*, a women's magazine, and *Saptahik Hindustan*, a weekly newsmagazine, and currently co-edits *Hindustan*, a daily newspaper, all published in Hindi, the first by the Times of India Group, and the latter two by *The Hindustan Times*. She has four plays, two novels, and four volumes of short fiction, among other works, to her credit. Her honours include the Om Prakash Sahitya Samman for her short stories in 1982.

K. AYYAPPA PANIKER, who also writes under the pen-name Tulasi, was born in Kerala in 1930. He received his M.A. in English from Kerala University, Trivandrum, and another M.A. and a Ph.D. from Indiana University, Bloomington. He has taught literature at various colleges and at Kerala University for about three decades, and currently teaches at the Institute of English at the University of Kerala. He edits *Medieval Indian Literature* for the Sahitya Akademi, New Delhi, as well as *Kerala kavita*, a poetry magazine. His work ranges over poetry, criticism, and scholarly and editorial projects in English and Malayalam, as well as translations from Malayalam into English. Among his publications are *A Short History of Malayalam Literature* (1977), a scholarly study in

English; *Ayyappa panikerude kritikal* (1974), a collection of poems in Malayalam, for which he won the Kerala state Sahitya Akademi award; and *Selected Poems of Ayyappa Paniker* (1985), a volume of poems in English and in English translation.

SUMITRANANDAN PANT, who was born in 1900 and died in 1977, became one of the principal figures in the 'romantic' *chhayavad* movement in Hindi in the second quarter of the twentieth century. He published poetry, short stories, and radio plays, and worked as chief producer at All India Radio.

RAJAGOPAL PARTHASARATHY was born in Tirupparaiturai, in Tamil Nadu, in 1934. He was educated at Siddhartha College, Bombay, and Leeds University in England. He taught English literature in Bombay in the 1960's, and worked as an editor for Oxford University Press in Madras and New Delhi in the 1970's and early 1980's. He then moved to the United States and completed a Ph.D. at the University of Texas, Austin. He teaches at Skidmore College in New York state. Among his publications are *Rough Passage* (1976), poems in English; *Ten Twentieth-Century Indian Poets* (1976), an edited anthology of Indian English poetry; and *The Cilappatikaram of Ilanko Atikal* (1993), an English translation of the Tamil classic. He was a visitor at the Iowa International Writing Program in 1978–9.

RAJANI PARULEKAR was born in Paras, Ratnagiri district, Maharashtra, in 1945. She received her M.A. from Elphinstone College, Bombay, and teaches Marathi literature at Burhani College there. Her collection of long narrative poems, *Dirgha kavita* (1985), won a Maharashtra state award. Her new book, *Kahi dirgha kavita*, appeared in 1993.

GIEVE PATEL was born in Bombay in 1940. He was trained at Grant Medical College, and worked at a rural health centre for three years before setting up his own practice in general medicine in Bombay. He is also an important contemporary Indian painter, and his works are included in private and museum collections in India, Europe, and America. His publications include essays on Indian art, translations from Gujarati, and plays and books of poetry in English, among them *Poems* (1966) and *How Do You Withstand, Body* (1976). He was awarded a Woodrow Wilson fellowship in 1989 for work in the theatre.

RAVJI PATEL was born in 1939 and studied humanities in Ahmedabad. He died after a short illness in 1968, and was awarded the Umasneharashmi Paritoshik posthumously. He wrote poems, short stories, and novelistic fiction, making extensive use of Gujarati folk materials and dialects. Gieve Patel's English translation of one of his famous poems, 'In Memory of Hushilal,' is available in *Poetry India*, vol. 2, no. 2.

CHANDRASHEKHAR BASAVARAJ PATIL was born in Hattimatur, Dharwar district, Karnataka, in 1939. He received an M.A. in English literature from Karnataka University in 1962, and a diploma in English studies from the Central Institute of English and Foreign Languages, Hyderabad, in 1969. He also earned an M.A. in linguistics and English language teaching from the University of Leeds, England. He has taught English at Karnataka University, Dharwar, for more than two decades. He writes poetry and plays in Kannada, and has edited *Sankramana*, a monthly magazine. Among his dozen publications are *Gandhi-smarane* (1976) and *O enna desha bandhavare* (1977), both volumes of poems. He received the Karnataka state Sahitya Akademi award for poetry in 1960 and for drama in 1974.

SIDDHALINGA PATTANSHETTI was born in Yadwad, Dharwar district, Karnataka, in 1939, and received his M.A. from Karnataka University in 1963. He has taught Hindi at Karnataka College, Dharwar. He writes in both Kannada and Hindi, and has published about two dozen books. These include translations of Saratchandra Chatterji' Bengali novels and of Mohan Rakesh and Dharamvir Bharati's Hindi plays into Kannada; short fiction in Kannada; and poetry in Hindi and Kannada. Among his collections of Kannada poems are *Nuraru padyagalu* (1977) and *Pratikshe* (1979).

DAYA PAWAR was born near Ahmednagar, Maharashtra, in 1935. He was trained as an accountant and is currently a senior auditor with the Western Railways in Bombay. He has been a prominent writer and intellectual in the Dalit movement in Maharashtra since 1967. His autobiographical fiction, *Baluta* (1978), is considered a classic Dalit narrative, and has been made into a film. His collection of poems, *Kondawada* (1974), won the Maharashtra government poetry award.

SALEEM PEERADINA was born in Bombay in 1944, and educated at the University of Bombay and at Wake Forest University, North Carolina, in the United States. He has taught in colleges since the early 1970's, and has served as the director of the Sophia Open Classroom in Bombay. He moved to the United States in the late 1980's, where he is currently the head of the English Department at Siena Heights College in Adrian, Michigan. He has edited an anthology, *Contemporary Indian Poetry in English* (1972), and published two collections of poems in English, *First Offence* (1980) and *Group Portrait* (1990).

N. PICHAMURTI was born in 1900 and died in 1978. Since his Telugu-speaking family had migrated early in the eighteenth-century to the Tamil region, he considered Telugu his mother tongue but chose to write in Tamil. As a member of the Congress Party, he was active in regional and national politics for over four decades. His published literary work includes several collections each of poetry and short fiction, as well as a novel and a play.

AMRITA PRITAM was born in Gujranwala, now in Pakistan, in 1919. Her mother, a school teacher, died when Pritam was eleven years old. Pritam started writing early and published her first book of poems, *Thandiyan kirnan* (1935), when she was sixteen. At that age she also married Gurbaksh Singh, to whom she had been engaged at age four, and with whom she had two children. This marriage, however, ended in divorce in 1960. Since 1947 Pritam has lived in New Delhi. She was the first woman writer to win the national Sahitya Akademi award, which she received for *Sunhare*, a book of poems, in 1956. She has published more than seventy books in Punjabi, including twenty-eight novels, eighteen collections of poetry, five volumes of short stories, and an autobiography. Her selected poems in Punjabi, with Hindi and English translations, are available in *Chuni hui kavitaen* and

Selected Poems, both published in 1982. Among other translated works are *Revenue Stamp* (1976), her autobiography, *Black Rose* (1968), a novel, and *The Skeleton and Other Stories.* Her honours include the Government of India's Padma Shri award in 1969; an honorary D.Litt. from the University of Delhi in 1973; the international Vaptsarov Award given by the government of Bulgaria, in 1980; and the Bharatiya Jnanapith award in 1981. She has also been a nominated member of the Rajya Sabha, the upper house of Indian Parliament.

WILLIAM RADICE, born in 1951, attended Westminster School, and studied English at Magdalen College, Oxford. He received a diploma in Bengali from the School of Oriental and African Studies, London (where he is now a lecturer in Bengali), and a D.Phil. from Oxford, for research on the Bengali poet Michael Madhusudan Dutt. He has published three books of poems, and has translated Rabindranath Tagore *Selected Poems* (1987) and *Selected Short Stories* (1991).

SAVITHRI RAJEEVAN was born in 1955 and lives in Trivandrum, Kerala, where she works on the editorial staff of *Samskar Keralam,* a journal. Her poetry has appeared in various Malayalam magazines, as well as in anthologies like *Puthukavithakal* and *Tiranjetutha 51 kavithakal.*

B.C. RAMACHANDRA SHARMA was born in Bangalore, Karnataka, in 1925. He earned his B.Sc. and B.Ed. degrees from Mysore University, and went on to receive B.Sc. and Ph.D. degrees in psychology from the University of London. He has lived and worked in India, England, Ethiopia, Malawi, and Zambia, among other countries. He is a bilingual writer in Kannada and English, and has published more than fifteen books since the 1950's. These include his own poetry in English, English versions of his Kannada poems, and Kannada translations of modern poetry in English. His Kannada works include a radio play, short stories, and several volumes of verse, among them *Hesaragatte* (1969) and *Brahmana huduga* (1977). He has recently edited an anthology of contemporary Kannada short stories in English translation.

ATTIPAT KRISHNASWAMI RAMANUJAN was born in Mysore, Karnataka, in 1929, and died in Chicago in 1993. He was educated in Mysore, and taught at colleges in Baroda, Belgaum, Quilon, and Pune in the 1950's. In 1959 he went to the United States and earned his Ph.D. in linguistics from Indiana University, Bloomington. Between 1962 and 1993 he taught mainly at the University of Chicago, where at the time of his death, he was the William E. Colvin Professor in the Department of South Asian Languages and Civilizations, the Department of Linguistics, the Committee on Social Thought, and the College. His collections of poetry in English are *The Striders* (1966), *Relations* (1971), and *Second Sight* (1986); and his books of poems in Kannada are *Hokkulallai huvilla* (1969) and *Mattu itara padygalu* (1977). Among his works of translation are *The Interior Landscape* (1967), *Hymns for the Drowning* (1981) and *Poems of Love and War* (1985), from Tamil; *Speaking of Siva* (1973) and U.R. Anantha Murthy's *Samskara* (1976), from Kannada; and *Folktales from India* (1992). His collected poems appeared in 1995 and his collected essays are forthcoming in 1997.

BHANUJI RAO, born in Cuttack in 1926, received his B.A. from Utkal University in 1949. He has worked as a journalist and a teacher. Between 1958 and 1969, he served on the editorial staff of *Matrubhumi* and *Kalinga*, both Oriya newspapers. In the 1970's and early 1980's he was a teacher of Oriya and Bengali at the Lal Bahadur Shastri National Academy of Administration, Mussoorie, Uttar Pradesh. Among his books of poetry are *Nutan kavita* (1955) and *Bishada eka rutu* (1973).

PARESH CHANDRA RAUT was born in Cuttack, Orissa, in 1936. He received an M.A. in English from the University of Delhi, and teaches literature at Ravenshaw College, Cuttack. His collections of poems in Oriya include *Mrityura pratibhi* (1981).

SUNIL B. RAY was born in Dhaka, now in Bangladesh, in 1916. He was a member of the Indian Administrative Service for more than thirty years. Since his retirement, he has translated extensively from French, German, Spanish, Persian and Urdu into Bengali, and from Bengali into English, French, German, and Persian.

P.S. REGE was born in Ratnagiri district in the Konkan region of Maharashtra, in 1910. He studied economics in Bombay and London in the 1930's. He taught economics at various colleges in Maharashtra and Goa, and retired in the 1970's as principal of Elphinstone College, Bombay. His work in Marathi includes eight books of poems, two collections of short fiction, three novels, and two volumes of essays and criticism. Among his later collections of poetry are *Dusara pakshi* (1966), *Priyala* (1972), and *Suhrdgatha* (1975), the last a volume of selected poems. He died in 1978.

NINDUMANURI REVATHI DEVI was born in Tenali, Andhra Pradesh, in 1951. She had an M.A. in philosophy and was completing a doctoral dissertation on Jean-Paul Sartre at Sri Venkateswara University, Tirupati, when she ended her own life in 1981. Her poems, written in Telugu, were collected and published posthumously in *Shilalolitha* (1981).

DAVID RUBIN teaches in New York. He has translated the selected poems of Suryakant Tripathi (Nirala) from Hindi and of Lakshmikant Devkota from Nepali, and has published a book on the Hindi-Urdu fiction writer, Munshi Premchand. His recent scholarly work includes *After the Raj: British Novels of India Since 1947* (1988).

PADMA SACHDEV, born in Jammu in 1940, works as a staff artist for All India Radio, Bombay. She has published several books of poetry in Dogri, and two of prose in Hindi. Her volume of Dogri poems, *Meri kavita, mere geet* (1969), won the national Sahitya Akademi award in 1971.

RAGHUVIR SAHAY was born in Lucknow, Uttar Pradesh, in 1929, and was educated at Lucknow University, which granted him an M.A. in 1951. He worked in New Delhi mostly as a journalist and an editor, from the early 1950's until his death in 1990. He was assistant editor of *Pratik* in 1951–2, and co-editor of *Kalpana* in 1957–8. He served as a special correspondent at All India Radio, New Delhi, between 1959 and 1963, and at *Navbharat Times*, a Hindi newspaper, between

1963 and 1968. He was editor of *Dinman*, a Hindi newsweek-
ly, during 1971–82, and subsequently an assistant editor at
Navbharat Times. He published more than ten books, includ-
ing *Atmahatya ke viruddha* (1967), *Hanso hanso jaldi hanso*
(1975), and *Kuch pate kuch chithiyan* (1989), all volumes of
poetry. He also published collections of essays and short
stories, and translated Shakespeare's *Macbeth* into Hindi for
the National School of Drama, New Delhi.

INDIRA SANT was born in Pune, Maharashtra, in 1914. In the
mid-1930's she married N.M. Sant, also a young Marathi
poet, who died after a bout of typhoid in 1946 and left her
a widow at a young age. For the next three decades Indira
Sant supported herself and her children by working full-time
as a teacher in Belgaum, retiring in the 1970's as the prin-
cipal of a teacher's training college. During this period she
wrote fiction for children as well as nearly five hundred
poems. Her collections of poetry include *Ranagbavari*
(1964), *Shela* (1966), *Mendi* (1967), *Bahulya* (1972), and
Garbhareshim (1982). Her selected poems are available in
Mrnmayi (1981), edited by Ramesh Tendulkar, and English
translations by Vrinda Nabar and Nissim Ezekiel are
gathered in *Snake-skin and Other Poems* (1975).

K. SATCHIDANANDAN was born in 1946. He has been a professor
of English at Christ College, Irinjalakuda, Kerala, and is
currently the editor of *Indian Literature* at the Sahitya
Akademi, New Delhi. He has translated the plays of W.B.
Yeats and Bertolt Brecht and the poetry of Pablo Neruda,
Zbigniew Herbert, and others into Malayalam. Among his
eleven volumes of poetry in Malayalam are *Anchu suryan*
(1971) and *Atmagita* (1972). He has also published a collec-
tion of plays, *Sakthan thampuram*, and seven books of literary
criticism, among them *Kurukshetran* (1970).

SARVESHWAR DAYAL SAXENA was born in Basti, Uttar Pradesh, in
1927, and died in 1984. He received an M.A. from Allahabad
University, and worked initially as an assistant producer at
All India Radio. He was on the editorial staff of *Dinman*, a
weekly newsmagazine in Hindi, for nearly two decades,
before serving as the editor of *Parag*, a Hindi magazine for

children. Besides poetry, he wrote plays, novels, and short stories. Among his twenty books are *Kuano Nadi* (1974) and *Jangal ka dard* (1976), both collections of poems. He was invited by the Soviet Writers' Union to the Pushkin Poetry Symposium in 1972. His other honours include the Authors' Guild award in 1978, the Madhya Pradesh government's Tulsi Puraskar in 1979, and the Delhi Sahitya Kala Parishad award in 1981.

CLINTON B. SEELY has been teaching Bengali and Indian literatures at the University of Chicago since the 1970's. He has translated Ramparshad's eighteenth-century lyrics, Michael Madhusudan Dutt's poetry from the nineteenth century, and Jibanananda Das's poems from the twentieth. Among Seely's recent publications is *A Poet Apart* (1990), a literary biography and study of Das.

MARTHA ANN SELBY, born in Nevada, Iowa, in 1954, recently completed her doctoral studies in South Asian languages and literatures at the University of Chicago. Her scholarly interests range over Sanskrit, Prakrit, and Tamil. She has translated the Prakrit *Gathasaptashati* into English, and currently teaches at Southern Methodist University, Texas.

VIKRAM SETH was born in Calcutta in 1952. He attended schools in India and England, and received his subsequent education at Corpus Christi College, Oxford, and Stanford University, California. At Stanford, he worked in economics as well as creative writing. He has published an award-winning travelogue about Tibet, *From Heaven Lake* (1983); a full-length novel in verse, *The Golden Gate* (1986); and a long best-selling novel in prose, *A Suitable Boy* (1993). His recent collections of poems include *The Humble Administrator's Garden* (1985) and *All You Who Sleep Tonight* (1990). He won the Commonwealth Poetry Prize in 1986 and the national Sahitya Akademi award in 1988.

SHAHRYAR is the pen-name of Akhlaq Mohammad Khan, who was born in Anwala, Bareilly district, Uttar Pradesh, in 1936. He was educated in Bulandshahr and at Aligarh Muslim University, Uttar Pradesh. He has worked as a lecturer in Urdu, on the editorial staff of *Anjuman Tariqqi-e-Urdu*, and at the library of Guru Nanak Dev University, Amritsar. He has been the editor of the *Ghalib* fortnightly, and the assistant editor of *Hamari zaban*. Among his collections of poetry in Urdu are *Satwan dar* (1970) and *Hijra-ke-mosam* (1978), and the latter received the Uttar Pradesh Academy award.

G. SHANKARA KURUP was born into a poor family in Nayathode, a village near Kalady, Kerala, in 1901. He studied Malayalam, Sanskrit, and English in high school, and his only higher academic qualification was the title of *vidwan* (scholar) from the University of Madras. He taught in various educational institutions in Cochin (Kerala) for fifteen years, before becoming a tutor, and subsequently professor of Malayalam, at Maharaja's College, Ernakulam, from where he retired in 1956. He then worked for a while as a producer at All India Radio, Trivandrum, and between 1968 and his death in 1972, he served as a nominated member of the Rajya Sabha, the upper house of Indian Parliament. Shankara Kurup's writing passed through nationalistic, radically progressive, and mystical-symbolic (including Vedantic) phases. Among his important collections of poetry are *Sahitya kautukam* (four volumes, 1923–); *Odakkuzhal* (1950), for which he won the first Jnanpith Award, India's highest literary honour; and *Vishwadarshanam* (1960), for which he received the Kerala state Sahitya Akademi award. Besides more than fifteen volumes of poetry, Shankara Kurup published five plays; four collections of essays; an autobiography; and Malayalam translations of Omar Khayyam, Kalidasa, Bhasa and Tagore.

GHULAM MOHAMMED SHEIKH was born in Surendranagar, Saurashtra, Gujarat, in 1937. He is a poet in Gujarati as well as a painter. He studied art at the School of Fine Arts, University of Baroda, and the Royal College of Art, London. He is now the head of the Department of Painting and teaches painting and aesthetics at M.S. University, Baroda. Between 1969 and 1973 he was one of the editors of *Vrishchik*, a cultural magazine in English. His paintings have been exhibited at the Centre Georges Pompidou, Paris, and the Art Institute, Chicago. His Gujarati poems are collected in *Athawa* (1974). He received the Government of India's Padma Shri award in 1983.

GUGGARI SHANTHAVERAPPA SHIVARUDRAPPA, was born in Shikar-pur, Shimoga district, Karnataka, in 1926, and received his M.A. (1953) and Ph.D. (1960) from Mysore University. Since then he has taught and conducted research on Kannada literature at various institutions, including Osmania University and Bangalore University. He has published nearly twenty books in Kannada, including works of criticism, aesthetics, travel, and poetry. His *Moscowdalli ippatteradu dina*, a travelogue, won the Soviet Land–Nehru award in 1973. Among his collections of poems is *Gode* (1972).

KEDARNATH SINGH was born in Chakia, Uttar Pradesh, in 1934. He was educated at Banaras Hindu University, from where he received an M.A. in Hindi literature in 1956 and a Ph.D. in 1964. He has taught at U.P. College, Varanasi, and St. Andrew's College, Gorakhpur, and has served as the principal of U.N. Postgraduate College, Pandrauma, Uttar Pradesh. Since 1978 he has been a professor of Hindi at the School of Languages, Jawaharlal Nehru University, New Delhi. He has published two books of scholarly criticism on modern Hindi literature, as well as several volumes of poetry, including *Zamin pak rahi hai* (1980); *Pratinidhi kavitaen* (1985), selected poems; and *Akal mein saras* (1988).

SHAMSHER BAHADUR SINGH, who wrote in Hindi and Urdu, was born in Dehradun, Uttar Pradesh, in 1911, and received a B.A. from Allahabad University in 1953. He worked as a bibliographer in Hindi, Urdu, Persian, and other languages. Between the early 1940's and the late 1970's he published more than fifteen books, among them collections of essays, sketches, stories, and poems. His selected early and late poems are available in *Chuka bhi hun nahin main* (1975), which won the Sahitya Akademi award as well as the Madhya Pradesh Sahitya Parishad's Tulsi Puraskar in 1977. His recent collection is *Itane paas apne* (1980). He died in 1993.

KABITA SINHA, who also writes under the pen-names Kabita and Sultana Choudhury, was born in Calcutta in 1931. She was educated at Presidency College and Ashutosh College, Calcutta. She joined All India Radio in 1965 and is currently the station director in Darbhanga, Bihar. Since the early

1950's she has published nearly twenty books in Bengali. Among them are several novels and volumes of poetry, and a collection of short stories. Her recent works include *Kabita parameshwari* (1976), *Horina boiri* (1985), and *Shreshto kabita* (1987), books of poetry, the last a selection; and *Momer tajmahal* (1989), a biography of her grandmother written in a nineteenth-century Bengali autobiographical style. She won Calcutta University's Lila Prize in 1976, and was a visitor at the Iowa International Writing Program in 1981–2.

SRI SRI, whose real name was Srirangam Srinivasa Rao, was born in Visakhapatnam, Andhra Pradesh, in 1910, and died in 1983. He started writing poetry and fiction while still in school, and over more than five decades he was associated with various movements and styles in Telugu, such as the Bhavakavitvam school (romantic poetry), nationalistic poetry, progressive poetry, and surrealism and experimentalism. He translated Baudelaire's poems into Telugu in the 1930's; and Andre Breton's surrealist manifesto and the poems of Paul Eluard, Apollinaire, and Salvador Dali in the 1940's. Sri Sri collected his progressive poems in *Mahaprasthanam* (1950), and his surrealist and experimental poems in *Khadga srishti* (1966). Besides poetry, he published critical essays, journalistic articles, satires, experimental plays and short stories, all of which are available in the six-volume *Sri sri sahityamu* (1972), collected works in Telugu. Among his honours were the Sahitya Akademi award (1972), the Soviet Land–Nehru award, and the Rajyalakshmi Foundation Award (1979).

NARAYAN SURVE, was born around 1926. Orphaned or abandoned soon after birth, he grew up in the streets of Bombay, sleeping on the pavements and earning a meagre livelihood by doing odd jobs and wage labour. He taught himself to read and write, and published his first book of poems, *Majhe vidyapith*, in 1966. He has since been associated with the Workers' Union Movement and has supported himself as a school teacher in Bombay. His second collection of poems, *Jahirnama*, appeared in 1978. In the 1970's Surve was often championed in India as well as in the Soviet Union and various Eastern Bloc countries as a 'truly proletarian' poet. English versions of his early poems are available in *On the Pavements of Life* (1973).

RABINDRANATH TAGORE was born in Calcutta in 1861, the fourteenth child of Debendranath Tagore, the head of the Brahmo Samaj. Rabindranath was educated by private tutors at home, and started writing at an early age. His collected works in Bengali fill twenty-six large volumes, and include about sixty collections of verse, among them *Gitanjali*; novels like *Gora* and *The Home and the World*; a large number of short stories, including 'Kabuliwallah'; a body of experimental plays, among them *The Post Office* and *Red Oleanders*; and short and long essays on a range of literary, social, cultural, political, and philosophical themes. His own English translations of his works are available in *Collected Poems and Plays of Rabindranath Tagore* (1936). New versions of his poems and stories are to be found in *Selected Poems* (1985) and *Selected Short Stories* (1992), both prepared by William Radice. Tagore was also a composer, musician, and song-writer and wrote nearly two thousand songs that have become the national music of Bengal, among which are the national anthems of India and Bangladesh; in old age, he became a remarkable painter. He founded and funded Vishwa Bharati, the international school and university at Shantiniketan, about one hundred miles northwest of Calcutta. He won the Nobel Prize for literature in 1913 and died in 1941.

SUNANDA TRIPATHY was born in Raghunathpura, Orissa, in 1964. She holds a master's degree in Sanskrit and a bachelor's degree in law. She has taught Sanskrit at Pipili College, Puri, and has also worked in Puri as a journalist.

S. USHA, who was born in Mysore in 1954, teaches Kannada literature in Karnataka and is editorially associated with a literary magazine, *Samvada*. Her two collections of poetry are *Togalu gombeya atmakathe* (1981), which won the Udayonmukha Vardhaman prize in 1986, and *Ee nelada hadu* (1990), which received the Karnataka state Sahitya Akademi award that year.

VAIDEHI is the pen-name of Janaki Srinivas Murthy, who was born in Kundapura in Dakshina Kannada district, Karnataka, in 1945. She writes prose as well as verse in Kannada, and has published one award-winning novel, *Asprushyaru* (1982); four volumes of short stories, including *Antaragada putagula* (1984) and *Gola* (1986); and five plays for children. She has translated into Kannada two important feminist works, Kamaladevi Chattopadhyay's *Indian Women's Struggle for Freedom* (1983) and Maitraiyee Mukhopadhyay's *Silver Shackles* (1985). Her collection of poems in Kannada is *Bindu bindige* (1990).

SHRIKANT VERMA was born in Bilaspur, Madhya Pradesh, in 1931. He was educated there and in Raipur and at Nagpur University, from where he received an M.A. in Hindi in 1956. He then moved to Delhi, where he worked as a journalist and in political organizations. During 1966–77 he was a special correspondent for *Dinman*, and in 1976 he became an elected member of the Rajya Sabha, the upper house of the Indian Parliament. During the late 1970's and early 1980's, he was an official and spokesman of the Congress (I) Party under Mrs Indira Gandhi's leadership. Verma died in New York in 1986. He published nearly twenty books in Hindi, including a novel and collections of short stories, essays, interviews with writers, and poems. His important collections of poetry are *Jalsaghar* (1973) and *Magadh* (1984). His honours include visits to the Iowa International Writing Program (1970–1 and 1978), and the Madhya Pradesh Government's Tulsi Puraskar in 1976.

CAROLYN WRIGHT has published four collections of poetry. She also translates poetry from Spanish and, with collaborators, from Bengali. She worked on contemporary Bengali women's poetry while she was in Calcutta on an Indo-US subcommission grant in 1986–8. She was in Dhaka, Bangladesh, as a Fulbright scholar in 1989–91.

SITANSHU YASHASHCHANDRA was born in Bhuj, in the Kutch region of Gujarat, in 1941. He received M.A. and Ph.D. degrees in Gujarati and Sanskrit from the University of Bombay; and an M.A. in aesthetics and a Ph.D. in comparative literature from Indiana University, Bloomington. He was a Fulbright scholar in 1968 and a Ford West European fellow in 1971. He was the chief editor of the Sahitya Akademi's *Encyclopaedia of Indian Literature* between 1976 and 1982, and since then he has been a professor of Gujarati at M.S. University, Baroda. His publications include several plays; *Odysseusnum halesum* (1975) and *Mohenjo daro* (1976), both volumes of poetry; and *Simankan ane simollanghan* (1977), a book of theory and criticism. Among his honours are the Nanalal award and the Gujarat state government poetry award in 1975–6.

ARLENE R.K. ZIDE, a linguist, poet, translator, and editor, teaches languages and humanities at Harold Washington College, Chicago. She is a co-editor of *Primavera*, a journal of women's writing. With the Oriya writer Jagannath Prasad Das, she has published *Under a Silent Sun* (1992), translations of recent Oriya women's verse. She has also edited *In Their Own Voice* (1993), an anthology of contemporary Indian women's poetry.

ELEANOR ZELLIOT received her Ph.D. from the University of Pennsylvania, where she wrote a dissertation on Dr Ambedkar and the Dalit movement in Maharashtra. She has taught history and Indian studies at Carleton College, Minnesota, for more than fifteen years. She has published widely on the Dalit literature, culture, and politics, and on the history and anthropology of Maharashtra.

Index of Languages, Poets, and Translators

III. TRANSLATORS

Copyright Statement

'Lifetime' by Narayan Surve
'Towards Delhi' by Kunwar Narain

Vagartha (New Delhi), for:
'Drought' by Sitanshu Yashashchandra
'Fire' by Amiya Chakravarty
'Genesis' by K. Satchidanandan
'Jaisalmer, 1' by Ghulam Muhammed Sheikh
'Calcutta and I' by Sunil Gangopadhyay

Baidar Bakht and Kathleen Grant Jaeger, ed. and trans., *An Anthology of Modern Urdu Poetry*, vol. 1 (Delhi: Educational Publishing House, 1984), for:
'Morsel' by Ali Sardar Jafri
'Tall Buildings' by Munib-ur-Rahman

Indian Council for Cultural Relations (New Delhi), for translations from the following publications:
Indian Poetry Today, 4 vols. (ICCR, 1974–81):
'Compromise' by Akhtar-ul-Iman
'Humiliation' by Kaifi Azmi
'Husband' by Popati Hiranandani
'Still Life' by Shahryar
'Whirlwind' by Ravji Patel
'Rice' by Chemmanam Chacko
'I and "I"' by Khalil-ur-Rahman Azmi
'This Man' by G.S. Shivarudrappa
Shrikant Verma, ed., *Poetry Festival India* (ICCR, 1985):
'Forgive Me' by Shakti Chattopadhyay

Adil Jussawalla, ed., *New Writing in India* (Harmondsworth: Penguin, 1974), for:
'Salutations' by Shanmuga Subbiah
'National Bird' by N. Pichamurti

Keki N. Daruwalla, *Indian English Poetry, 1960–1980* (Delhi: Vikas, 1980), for:
'My Father Travels' by Dilip Chitre

Vikram Seth, *All You Who Sleep Tonight* (New York: Alfred Knopf, 1990), for:

'A Doctor's Journal Entry for August 6, 1945' by Vikram Seth

Adil Jussawalla, *Missing Person* (Bombay: Clearing House, 1976), for:

'Sea Breeze, Bombay' by Adil Jussawalla

Sitakant Mahapatra, *Old Man in Summer and Other Poems* (Calcutta: United Writers, 1975), for:

'The Election' by Sitakant Mahapatra

Pritish Nandy, for:

'The Task' by Subhash Mukhopadhyay

Nirendranath Chakrabarti, *The Naked King and Other Poems*, trans. Sujit Mukherjee and Meenakshi Mukherjee (Calcutta: Writers Workshop, 1975), for:

'Amalkanti' by Nirendranath Chakrabarti

Gieve Patel, for:

'Forensic Medicine' by Gieve Patel

Orient Longman (New Delhi), for:

'To My Daughter' by N. Balamani Amma

Translation (New York), for:

'The Diamond of Character' by Kabita Sinha

Arlene Zide and Penguin Books India Ltd (New Delhi), for:

'The Girl's Desire Moves Among Her Bangles' by Gagan Gill
'Woman, 2' by Jyotsna Milan
'Man' by Archana Varma
'Two Women Knitting' by Mrinal Pande
'The Creative Process' by Amrita Pritam
'A Pair of Glasses' by Savithri Rajeevan
'Tryst' by Sunanda Tripathy

Agyeya [S.H. Vatsyayan], *Signs and Silence* (Delhi: Simant, 1976), for:

'Hiroshima' by Agyeya